KONKERER

By Robb 'FrostByte' King

Copyright © 2013
Robert J. King, Jr.
All Rights Reserved

No part of this book may be used, reproduced or duplicated without the permission of the author or publisher.

Published by Syre Arts & Greater Is He Publishing
Cleveland, Ohio

Cover Design: Syre Grafix
Cover Photo: Sherman Stewart
Additional Edits: Tracey Wiley

ISBN: 978-1-938950-26-1

Printed in USA by Greater Is He Publishing
9824 E. Washington St., Chagrin Falls, Ohio 44023
P.O. Box 46115, Bedford, Ohio 44146
http://www.greaterishepublishing.com

Office: 216.288.9315

For book signings and purchase information, contact Robb King at:

robbking76@hotmail.com
www.ig.com/@Syrearts
www.facebook.com/Robb Frostbyte King
www.twitter.com/frostbyte76

TABLE OF CONTENTS

Acknowledgments		1
Forward		3
Introduction		5
Chapter 1:	Fear and Mischief	6
Chapter 2:	4th Grade Blues	17
Chapter 3:	A Bout with Bullies	21
Chapter 4:	No Sleep	27
Chapter 5:	Evolving	33
Chapter 6:	To Be or Not to Be All I Can Be	37
Chapter 7:	Future Crushed	44
Chapter 8:	I Want to Go Away	51
Chapter 9:	Welcome to E.C.	60
Chapter 10:	Living… or Existing	71
Chapter 11:	Oh the Pain	77
Chapter 12:	Building a Blessing	90
Chapter 13:	Poetic Newness	99
Conclusion		106
Message to the Reader		109
About the Author		111

ACKNOWLEDGMENTS

Lord, thank you for your many blessings... for being my shield and allowing me to share my gifts. Momma, thanks for the many talks we shared during this writing process and for constantly reminding me that it's all in the past, I LOVE YOU. Stefan, Brian and Jaqui, I love you and admire you more than you'll ever know. My big sister Florenza, I thank God daily for finding you, I love you. To my family and friends (there's so many of you! LOL), I love you.

I would like to give a special shout-out to The Men of Destiny, Jerry Primm II (thanks for being a brother and friend), Tanya Lynne (the best counselor a man could have - I can't thank you enough).

Roeshana B., Jenetta D. (RIH), Regina K., Vigatron, Dani R. (RIH), Samantha, Tracey W., Shameka, Lamesa, Ahnesty, Trissa C., Iyesha, Kenya, Ase Boogie, BSAH (you know who you are! LOL), Strong Arm Security (Squad!!!), Shalana Satterwhite and Greater Is He Publishing - thank you so much. Since 2002, I've had the pleasure to meet and work with so many artists and received love from so many supporters. I appreciate all of you.

This book is dedicated to anyone in search of healing. Know that everything is going to be alright.

Remember... He's Working... Pay Attention.

Conquer [kóngkər]: 1. To defeat or subdue by force, especially by force of arms. 2. To gain or secure control. 3. To overcome or surmount by physical, mental, or moral force. Synonym: <u>Defeat</u>.

FOREWORD

Sharing your life story will encourage others to live. Its what God wants us to do. For we all have testimonies... some are more explicit than others. You also need to remember that some people will not embrace what you've shared about your life, including your dearest family and friends, for this process takes a lot of courage. It will take God's strength and shield to endure all the backbiting and criticism you'll encounter.

During this journey, I came to realize that all the pain and suffering I held on to for so long hindered me... making me mentally, physically, and spiritually ill. All those faded memories are like roots that seem to hide underground, waiting until the next spring season so they can sprout new memories. In the midst of all these memories, I became miserable... looking for some sort of sympathy. I had to realize that all company isn't good company; in fact, some people use your past against you instead of helping you recover.

It shouldn't take near-death experiences to make you look at life from a whole new perspective. This is what happened to me. Instead of living, I hid behind my 700 lb. shell, afraid to show the world who Bobby really was. Afraid to speak because I thought no one would listen. Afraid to reach goals because others told me I couldn't. I lived in fear... of success... of trying and failing... of conquering.

It took three weeks in the hospital to realize that I didn't have to live in fear because I had God on my side.

INTRODUCTION

Would you believe me if I told you that in my brush with death, I met an angel in the form of a nurse, who asked me if I knew how to dance? I asked him if he was serious and he replied, "Yes! Your life is a melody waiting to be played, and we're eager to hear your song. As the years have passed you by, you've been nodding your head to everyone else's tune. Since you won't play your own song, you might as well continue grooving to theirs. So, I'll ask you again... can you dance?"

I didn't give him an answer. I just stared at him as he took blood samples and checked my blood pressure. "Why does he care anyway?" I thought to myself. I was just one of many patients he'd service during his daily work routine. Many people seem to speak just to hear themselves talk, and back then everybody had something to say to or about me. To me, he was no different. He might as well have just said, "Get your fat ass up, get on a diet and exercise plan so you can lose that weight!" like everyone else did. As he walked out the door he looked at me and said, "Think about that, okay?" I never saw him again.

CHAPTER 1

Fear and Mischief

I could lie to you and say that my life was pretty easy and that I ate with a silver spoon. I could even say that I was a poor boy growing up and barely got a bite to eat, but that would also be a lie. In fact, I was just your average kid trying to find my way in this world. My parents were married, hard-working with good jobs, owned a two-family house in East Cleveland and provided the best for us... one big happy family... from the outside looking in.

King

For the first ten years of my life it was just my brother and I, playing like there was no tomorrow... full of energy and mischief. Although we got disciplined when we were bad, like every other kid, my father was much harder on me than he was on my brother. Maybe it was because I was the oldest and should've known better. By the time I was five, I feared him and wished he would go away.

My wish came true, but my mom had to suffer from it. I remember one day a woman called the house and told my mom that she wanted my dad. "YOU CAN HAVE HIM!!!" She barked at the phone as if the woman was actually there. I was too young to know that my dad was cheating on my mom. I just knew they weren't getting along and my dad had to go.

My mom and dad were separated for a year or so. I remember him living with the woman he'd left my mom for. Whenever my brother and I visited, she tried to be our mother. I remember her trying to put me on a diet because she felt I was getting fat. She would cut all my meals in half. I was a little rebellious even though I was afraid of my dad. Once, over her sister's house, she tried to make me give my brother half of a hotdog I was eating. I stuffed it in my mouth. She was so mad that she threatened to tell my father. I didn't even care.

Later that night, when we went to pick my father up from work, she told my dad how I had stuffed the hotdog in my mouth. I guess she was expecting my father to whip me. He just said, "Okay." She turned and glared at me as if to say, "Yeah you are going to get it when we get home!" When we got there my dad said, "Okay boys, time to get ready for bed." Even I was surprised I didn't get a whipping.

During my parent's separation, I started to become very mischievous. I was fighting and eating the other kids' lunches in Catholic school. I stole money out of my mother's purse to buy candy from the corner store. Once I stole a ten-dollar bill from her, bought candy and gave a few dollars to some of the kids in the neighborhood. One of the neighbors told my mother and I got a spanking from her. She also called my father... he just barked at me over the phone.

My grandmother, aunts and uncles lived upstairs from us, and without my father around it was a "tension free" zone. It was so much fun until my dad came over and caused friction. I remember my mom having a birthday party and several other fun events at the house. One event that sticks out the most is when my uncle Gary built a basketball hoop, put it on the garage and had a big basketball game.

It seemed like there were boys from all over the neighborhood in our backyard waiting for a chance to play. I watched the games from the upstairs back porch. I remember one of the guys yelling to a girl next door, "Hey Cynthia, give me a glass of water with some ice in it!" We had a ball until a 1976 Chevy Malibu sped through the driveway, forming a "Red Sea" of teenage boys who were upset because the game was ruined.

"Get the fuck away from my house!" my father growled as kids scattered from the backyard. I got scared and hid on the porch until he left. He made my uncle tear down the basketball hoop. After that event, my dad started to come over more often to make sure things stayed in order.

After a year of being apart, my mom and dad got back together which forced my grandmother to move out. I remember him explaining his reasons for coming back, "Boys need their fathers in their lives" he told me as he held me tight in his arms. He seemed so sincere. I stared into his eyes and hoped he would be nicer. I was somewhat glad he was back, but that didn't last long. After a week or two, it seemed like he was back to being a monster, and my mischief got worse. It seemed like my mother got a call from my teachers every other day.

My father renovated the upstairs unit for us to move in. During that time, he taught me about different tools and even made me stick close to him as he worked on the upstairs unit. I was his "gopher" so to speak, running to and fro in search of tools with names I'd never heard of.

"Hey Bobby, go in the basement and get my...." is what I constantly heard as soon as he got home from work. I would try to sneak away to watch television only to hear him yell, "Bobby, where the hell did you go?! Keep your ass over here!"

As we got settled upstairs, I started to become more responsible around the house. My mother worked second shift, so I had to watch my brother for a few hours until my father got home later in the evening. My brother was only three years younger, so we were watching each other. We were both very in tune with our surroundings. I guess when you add that to a little mischief, it made us sort of black versions of Dennis the Menace.

I remember one evening, while waiting on our dad to come home, we were heating up our mother's hot comb and blowing our hair out. We were astonished that we had afros. We were profiling in the bathroom mirror until we heard a buzzing noise in the television. It was our father talking on his CB radio, and also our way of knowing he was home. We started patting our hair back in and sat down like nothing ever happened. He never suspected a thing.

Over the next few years, my dad had become my nemesis. It seemed like he found any and every reason to chastise me. I wasn't making things any better with my mischief. I started stealing and lying at home and in school. I guess I was searching for attention from my father, whether it was good or bad.

By third grade, my mother took me out of Catholic school and sent me to Prospect Elementary in East

Cleveland. The beginning of the year went well, but I ended up carrying my bad ways to this school too. My teacher, Mrs. Wheat, was very short in height but was a "no nonsense" type. She didn't hesitate to give me a spanking. After a while, my mischievous ways started to subside. She would sit me down during recess, just talk to me and let me draw... things I enjoyed.

At home, the beatings got worse. My father decided to whip me with an extension cord. The first time was one weekend when my parents picked my uncle up to babysit us, so they could go out on a date. My father told us not to leave the backyard and that nobody could come in. At the time, we were accompanied by an older kid named Alonzo who lived around the corner. He was fixing the flat tires on our bikes.

While our parents were gone, a few boys from the neighborhood tried to climb over the gate and come into our backyard. I told them they weren't allowed but they proceeded anyway. One of them smacked me in the face, so I grabbed a baseball bat and chased them up the street. Alonzo followed suit on his bike and my brother watched from the front gate. As I swung the bat at the boys, my parents were turning the corner. I could see the anger in my father's eyes as he pulled into the driveway.

"I TOLD YOU NOT TO LEAVE THE YARD! You GOT A HARD ASS HEAD!"

KONKERER

I tried to explain what happened, but he wasn't on it. In his eyes I disobeyed him. Because my brother stood at the gate he only gave him a few taps on the buttocks, but I got whipped with the extension cord with no pants on. I was left with scars on my buttocks and the back of my legs. As the wounds began to heal, they started sticking to my underwear. My uncle was upset, but what could he do? He was just a teenager.

After a while, my mischief started to resurface. I was seeking attention and would do the dumbest stuff possible. My father would not only whip me, he would also sit and talk to me. In the midst of calling me a dummy, he would tell me why it wasn't right to be so bad. He'd always ask, "Bobby, why do you act up knowin' you gonna getcha ass whooped?"

All I could say was, "I dunno." Over time, he got frustrated with me constantly saying, "I dunno" and whipped me for saying that.

My attention span was less than a minute. If it didn't spark my interest, I would do other things that amused me like drawing, reading comic books or making people out of garbage bag ties. I was the same way in school. If what the teacher was teaching didn't interest me, I would just start drawing. My teachers would tell my parents I wasn't paying attention in school and that all I did was draw. My father got fed up and told me that I couldn't draw anymore. I would sneak around and draw anyway.

King

That year, my Christmas was horrible. I remember my brother Stef, my cousin Michelle (who was staying with us at the time) and me waking up to a beautifully decorated tree with toys and gifts all around it. There were gifts and toys for Stef and Michelle, but nothing for me. As they opened and played with their gifts, I just sat there and looked on in sadness.

When my father woke up he uncovered my gifts, which were hidden under a cover behind the tree. He stood there for a moment and told me the reason why I didn't get to open my gifts was because of my mischief. "Maybe next time you'll learn to do better so this won't happen again" he grumbled as he sat on the couch. I didn't get to open my gifts until a few weeks after the New Year.

When my aunt Julie moved in with us I didn't get into much trouble. She seemed to be my guardian angel. I remember her working at a bar called the Master Plan and the Townhouse Motel around the corner from our street. I would watch her as she walked up the street, and didn't go to sleep until she came home.

I tried not to get into much trouble when she was around. She had a delicate way of saying, "Now Bobby, you know that's not right. You don't want your father to spank you, do you?" I felt safe when she was around. Many a time she saved me from getting severe beatings.

It seemed my father would wait until my mother and

aunt were gone to find reasons to whip me. It could be anything, from our bedroom not being clean to him finding a finger smudge on the wall. As soon as he got home from work all you'd hear was, "BOBBY!!!" and I would run to see what he wanted. I could even hear his voice in my sleep.

At some point, I tried to be sneaky with my mischief. Sometimes I, along with some kids downstairs and others in the neighborhood, would go to the corner store and steal some candy or sweetened Kool-Aid packets. It was pretty easy. I remember once I went to the store with the girl that lived downstairs from us, and I stole a little bag of red cherry candy. When I showed her, she didn't say anything. About five minutes after we got home she said, "Bobby your father wants you!" I ran upstairs to see what he wanted, and before I could speak he knocked me upside the head with the phone receiver.

I touched my head and felt a bloody hole. He paused for a second and told the person that he was talking to, "Dammit lemme call you back. I done busted this boy's head open!" He grabbed a wet rag and placed it on my head and yelled, "See what you made me do!?! What the hell are you stealing for?!?" I couldn't answer. All I cared about was the gash in my head. He asked me what I had stolen. I pulled out the bag of candy. He shook his head and said, "Dammit I don't understand you! The older you get, the dumber you get!"

King

My father walked me to the corner store to tell the owner that I had stolen the candy. After paying for the candy, he decided to take me to the emergency room at Kaiser Permanente. You could tell it was hard for him to explain to the doctor why I had a gash in my head. I remember the doctor saying, "That was no reason to hit him like that!"

All my father could say was, "I know I know." The doctor put four stitches in and told us we could go. Before we walked out, the doctor whispered in my father's ear. I have no idea what he said, but my father let out a deep sigh.

On our way home, we talked about why I stole the candy. I told him that we did it all the time and I never told on her or any of the other kids. Later that night, I acted as if I was asleep when my mother and aunt came home. They both shed tears as they looked at my stitched noggin. I could hear my aunt telling my father that he had gone too far, that I knew better and deserved a spanking.

I couldn't understand why that girl would tell on me. It was something we did on a regular basis. I later realized that she, along with some other kids, found it humorous when we got spankings. They even imitated my father whipping us, "Boy... didn't... I... tell... you... not... to... do... that... again..." When people asked what happened, I'd lie and say that I was hit by a swing in the park.

My fear turned into hatred for my father. I'd wish that

KONKERER

he would die in a car crash on his way home from work. I even imagined him lying in a coffin, dressed quite dapperly in his light blue leisure suit. Seems crazy for an eight-year old to wish death on someone... right?

CHAPTER 2
4th Grade Blues

In October of my fourth-grade year, we moved to Warrensville Heights. My brother and I became schoolmates with our cousins, Adam and Marsha, at Westwood Elementary. On our first day, we had to take a placement test to see where we were academically. I didn't want to take the test, so I just went through each page and filled out the dots. The funny thing is that I understood the test, I was just being lazy.

My mother was so upset with me, she couldn't understand how I could do such a thing. I was searching for attention and it bit me in the butt. I was placed one class level above the Learning Disability class, and I hated it. The work was so easy that I got easily bored and would draw pictures of football players and comic book characters.

During parent/teacher conferences, my teachers would tell my mother that I couldn't comprehend what I was reading. I actually could, the work was just boring. I'd rather be mischievous instead. I remember getting into a fight with one of my fourth-grade classmates before the bus came to take us home. I won the fight. Another boy yelled out, "You think you're tough because you're from East Cleveland!"

I replied, "Yep, and I can beat all of y'all!"

As soon as I got off the morning bus the next day, all the boys from the fourth grade formed a lynch mob just to get a piece of me. The principal grabbed me and yelled, "What did you do to make all those boys want to fight you?" I told him that I had fought a boy the day before and the others got mad. While I was sitting in the principal's office, I could see one of the boys telling the principal that I said I could beat all the boys in the fourth grade. I wanted to beat him up. The principal came back into his office and scowled, "You'd better get yourself together young man! Nobody wants to be around a trouble maker!"

KONKERER

That year I joined the Cub Scouts. My uncle was one of the Pack leaders, and my cousin Adam was a fellow scout. I was a Cub Scout while I was in East Cleveland, but we didn't do much... maybe a park outing or Grand Prix car race here and there. Cub Scouts was very exciting, as there were so many activities to participate in.

I began to look up to my uncle. He was the type of father I'd always wanted, and he was very active in my cousin's life. My father decided to help out at the Cub Scout meetings. I was hoping it would make us closer. Nope... after one of our achievement ceremonies he threatened to whip me because I didn't achieve any badges or awards. "You've got to be the dumbest kid I know. Why in the hell you're the only one with no awards? Nigga, you better get on the stick or the stick will be whooping your ass!" That's what I heard on the way home.

That same year, my mother found out that she was pregnant. I was so excited that I told my teacher. He sat me down and told me that I had to become more responsible in everything I did. I tried to stay out of trouble from then on. I worked harder to achieve more merits in the Cub Scouts, and even surprised my teacher by earning a spot in the school spelling bee. He was amazed that I was the only one in my class to spell "achieve" correctly. Hmmm, I thank the Cub Scouts for that.

I also had to go to summer school that year in order to pass on to the fifth grade. Other than doing silly little things, like wearing my aunt's short-haired wig to school, I tried to be on my best behavior. My mother was due at any time, and we were hoping for a little sister. I remember drawing a family picture of us playing basketball.

I also joined the concert band playing the snare drum. My band director, Mr. Greible, was a young man fresh out of college. Within three months he taught me how to make music and not bang the snare head. I had my first band concert outside of Randallwood Middle School, along with my fellow classmates, who all played different instruments. We wore yellow t-shirts that said, "I survived my first band concert!"

On July 19th my brother Stef and I woke up to find our mother and father gone. Around 10:00 a.m., our father called home to let us know that mom was about to have the baby. Later that afternoon my father called and said, "Y'all have a little brother." Then five minutes later he called back and said, "And a little sister!" We cheered with joy... we had twins! My aunt picked us up and we spent the evening with our cousins. When my father picked us up later that night, he had the biggest smile on his face. "I leave with two kids and come back with four!" he bellowed.

CHAPTER 3
A Bout with Bullies

Fifth grade at Randallwood Middle School seemed like a whole new world with open classes. I was placed in a "self-contained" classroom because the teachers felt I would be distracted by the other classes. It seemed odd because I was in class with a few "straight A" students. Maybe we were the "ADHD" students of our time.

I won't say that fifth grade was a hard year. Academically I did pretty well, but my behavior was another story. There were a number of bullies in the sixth grade that pushed us around. I wasn't having it and decided to fight back. I would just watch them as they'd inflict fear in the other students, hoping they would start messing with me. I was kind of afraid of them, but my dad told me that bullies were nothing more than scary little punks. Once you stood up to them, they would leave you alone.

I remember there was a sixth-grader who would bully on both boys and girls. He was a chubby lad with the fattest cheeks I'd ever seen. I used to laugh at him because he reminded me of a chunkier version of Gary Coleman. I just knew he wouldn't bother me... I was wrong. One day during recess, he made a flying karate leap off the jungle gym and kicked me in the back. I just lay there on the ground in pain as he ran off laughing. Revenge was in order.

A few days later, I couldn't wait for recess. The anticipation brewed in me like coffee, and all I could see was my father's face taunting me. When the recess bell rang, I made haste to get outside. I saw him climbing the ladder of the jungle gym. Without a thought, I ran full speed towards him and kicked him in his butt. He flew off the ladder and fell face first onto the concrete. He just lay there screaming. I stood there and stared at him as he bled from a busted nose.

My heart was beating hard and fast. I knew that I was in trouble. Lucky for me, the only person that saw me kick him was a girl that he would often bully on. She told the recess monitors that she didn't see anything. We formed a friendship that lasted through high school. I didn't have to worry about another bully until sixth grade. This bully (let's call him Brandon) became a thorn in my side until I turned fifteen.

It seemed like every few months he found a reason to fight me, and it started to get old. He was very persistent; and no matter how bad you beat him he wanted more. I didn't want to fight him anymore, and it drove my brother nuts. He began to antagonize and make fun of Brandon every chance he got. A few of those sessions ended up with me fighting. I didn't want to, but it was either I protect my brother or get a beat down from my father... catch 22.

I remember playing football with some friends in our neighbor's backyard. One of the boys was kind of slow... okay, he was in a learning disability class. Brandon told him that I was making fun of his thick, pop bottle glasses. Even though it wasn't true, a fight broke out. I was winning until Brandon started to interfere with a push here and a punch there. Before I knew it, I was being double-teamed by both of them so I ran home.

The next morning on the bus the slow boy yelled out, "This fight ain't over Bobby!" I just ignored him. Every time I saw him, he would make a "fist in palm" gesture to constantly remind me that he was going to kick my butt. On the bus ride home, he kept staring at me. "I'm getting off at your bus stop!" he yelled.

"I ain't scared!" I replied. My plan was to punch him, then kick him in the crotch.

As soon as we got off the bus I punched him. He fell, then jumped back up and yelled, "Is that all you got?!" When he rushed me, I kicked him in both legs and then in his crotch. He fell over and yelled, "When I get up I'm kicking your ass!" I ran towards him with the intention of kicking him in the head, but I was tackled by Brandon. I got up and ran home. They followed and tried to open my screen door. I unlocked the screen door and rammed them both off the porch and into the bushes. My neighbor yelled at them and made them leave my yard. I was saved.

The next day in gym class the slow boy kept taunting me. "You're scared of me, aren't you?" he asked.

"Heck naw!" I replied. He kept bragging about how he chased me home twice. "No he didn't! He and Brandon tried to jump me!" I yelled. Several times the teacher had to tell us to settle down. The slow boy ignored her. After several more minutes of taunting, he walked behind me and put me in a head lock. I couldn't breathe, but I wasn't going to give up.

He let go when the teacher yelled. I turned around and punched him so hard that his glasses flew off. "Aaah, Mommy!!!" he screamed as he lay on the floor like a baby. I thought I was going to be in trouble, but the teacher assured the principal that I only reacted in self-defense. He never bothered me again. I wish I could say that about Brandon.

KONKERER

In the midst of going to school and dealing with bullies in sixth grade, I made tremendous progress. I was back on my grade level in reading and math, and was spelling on the seventh-grade level. My teachers were very proud of me. For the first time ever, my academics outweighed my behavior. The only changes I experienced at home were the two lovable babies. Physically, I started getting chunky and had low energy. I couldn't even beat my father in a race, and he had a big belly at the time.

My brother and I had our fair share of chores. During the summer we had to cut our grass, along with the neighbor's across the street, on account that my father stored his 1966 Cadillac Fleetwood Brougham in her garage. Likewise, in winter, we had to shovel our driveway along with hers. Back then, the snow would reach well over a foot and we cleared it like champs. Every now and then I got yelled at for not keeping up.

One day after school, my aunt wanted us to walk with her to Southgate Mall. We were told to have the back patio shoveled by the time my father got home. We didn't get home until fifteen minutes before he did. He looked out the kitchen window and said, "I thought I told y'all to shovel the back patio!" I responded by saying that we didn't have a chance to.

Before I could explain, he grabbed me and threw me on the ground. He put his foot on my chest and neck and picked up a chair. He roared, "DAMMIT I'LL KILL YOUR

DUMB ASS. WHEN I SAY SOMETHING, I MEAN IT!"

As he raised the chair over his head to strike me, aunt Julie ran up the stairs screaming, "I TOOK THEM WITH ME, THAT'S WHY THEY DIDN'T SHOVEL THE PATIO!!! LEAVE HIM ALONE!!!"

My father threw the chair down, took his foot off my chest and sat down. "Take y'all asses outside and shovel that damn patio!" he growled. My aunt saved my life, like she had a few times before. After we finished shoveling, I went to bed and cried. I couldn't understand how a man would want to hurt his child.

That year, my aunt Julie met a man and got married. She had the wedding in our house. I didn't want her to get married... I didn't want her to leave. I thought that when she left, there would be no one to protect me. The only good thing about aunt Julie leaving was that I got my own bedroom.

CHAPTER 4

No Sleep

My seventh-grade year was full of downs. It seemed like nothing was going right. I wasn't doing well in my classes except for English. The only thing I didn't like about that class was that my teacher kept calling me "Fred King", a student he'd had years before. My English teacher made us study poems and recite them. He also gave us writing assignments where we were able to use our imaginations. This is where I found my love for writing.

I had low self-esteem. You would've too if someone who was supposed to love and cherish you constantly called you a "dummy" and wished they would've killed you at birth. My mother always knew what to say to keep me encouraged. She even made me read Proverbs and Psalms for spiritual guidance. My family didn't do much to prevent my father's abuse. Maybe they didn't know what to do, didn't care or they feared him like I did. They'd just leave as soon as he got angry, then call a few hours later to see if anything happened.

Every night my baby brother and sister would make their way downstairs to my room and literally destroy it. Around the same time every night, I would hear them trotting down the stairs, trying to be quiet. Brian would always peek in, and I'd tell them to get back upstairs. This went on until I fell asleep. I would wake up the next morning with a bedroom that looked like a tornado hit it and a bed soaked in urine. Once, they busted a feather pillow and it took all year to get rid of the feathers.

If they weren't destroying my room, they were in the cabinets opening packs of Cream of Wheat, taking labels off the canned goods or spilling calamine lotion all over the place. My father would wake up and see what they'd done and scream my name to clean up the mess. Once, they opened a bag of cheese balls and had them everywhere. They even fed Stef and me some in our sleep. My father woke us up to clean the mess and made them eat the cheese balls. "And you bet not ask for water either!" he barked as he went back to bed. Brian asked anyway. So, as you can see, that's why I was barely able to sleep.

KONKERER

A year earlier, my aunt Gwen started picking me and Stef up for Sunday service at Holy Trinity Baptist Church. It was fun hearing Pastor Payden preach. He seemed so strong yet loving. I made sure I shook his hand after every service. A year later, I decided to join the church and get baptized. I remember my brother Stef, my cousin Gwen and me making what seemed like a long journey down the aisle. I prayed that this would help the situation with my father and other parts of my life, but it seemed like things got worse.

One of the neighbors told my father that I had torn up her flower bed because I was mad at her son. My father believed her. My mother came to my defense because she knew I liked flowers. My father hated that and found another reason to discipline me. He grabbed a fiberglass rod and whipped me until he got tired.

The whipping left wounds and blisters on the back of my thighs, and I was afraid to take gym. I was hoping the wounds would hurry up and heal because gym was the only time I could let off steam. During class, some blisters had burst and stuck to my pants. It was embarrassing to tell my teacher. She took me to the nurse and told my principal. The nurse put ointment on my wound, bandaged it and sent me to the principal's office.

Instead of going to the seventh-grade principal, I went to see Mr. Thomas, the assistant principal of the junior high. I told him about my wound and he wanted to talk to my parents. I told him whatever he did, not to call my father. He called my father anyway... at his job. I could hear my father barking through the phone. I started to cry because I knew I was in trouble. Soon after Mr. Thomas hung up the phone I yelled, "Why did you call my father?! I'm in big trouble now!"

Mr. Thomas told me to calm down and started telling jokes to make me feel better. Throughout my stay in junior high, he became my mentor. I could talk to him about anything. He even went to church with me.

Because of my wounds from the beatings, one of my aunts called family services. A counselor came over and asked several questions. One of the questions she asked was if I was afraid of my father. Without hesitation I said, "Yes!"

She came back over to meet my father. After several questions, she asked him if he believed that I was afraid of him. Without a blink he said, "No." She asked why, and he said, "If he was so afraid of me, he wouldn't do all that dumb shit." The counselor never came back, and I knew that if family services couldn't do anything, no one could.

You know what's funny? When I was nineteen, the truth came out about our neighbor's flower bed. One of my good friends blurted out, "I hated her. That's why I tore up her flowers!"

My father had a surprised look on his face and said, "What!?!" then looked at me. I just shook my head. He had a habit of beating us first and asking questions later.

KONKERER

I decided to join the wrestling team. A few of my friends were in peewee wrestling back in sixth grade. I thought wrestling was like WWF but found out different. Through wrestling I was able to find some discipline. In order for me to stay on the wrestling team, I had to be academically eligible. I tried my hardest to keep my grades up during the season.

One of my coaches, Mr. Vokac, favored Grizzly Adams. He was big, burly and moved like a cat... he even growled. He seemed very mean but had a heart of gold. He called me B.B. (like the Blues singer) and taught me how to handle pain. He showed me wrestling moves so I could handle guys bigger than me. He once told me that wrestling was more than a sport, it was a way of life... discipline.

After wrestling season was over, my grades started to fall. I had so many distractions, and I had a hard time sleeping. Not to mention that my cousin from Alabama had moved in months earlier. He slept in my bedroom. For about a year and a half, I slept on the couch in the basement. Several times we'd fought because he wouldn't let me enter my room. Living in that house left a bitter taste in my mouth.

In order to improve my grades, I tried studying and everything, but my mind was flooded with so much dismay. I got caught cheating in a few of my classes and had to take notes home to be signed by a parent. Because of my artistic ability, I forged my mother's name. Most of my teachers required that all failed tests be signed, and my mother got so fed up with me bringing F's home that she refused to sign another paper.

Besides my failing grades, I tried out for the school choir. It should've been a cinch since I was able to sing. During tryouts, the choir director asked me to sing "My Country, 'Tis of Thee." As I was singing, signs of puberty took over. My voice cracked and jumped to various octaves. I sounded like Alfalfa of the Little Rascals singing "Oh Suzanna." I wasn't good enough to get into the choir. That was the least of my worries.

I was sweating bullets wondering if I was going to pass or fail the seventh grade. My parents didn't get a notice stating that I needed to go to summer school, so I was really scared. That whole summer before my eighth-grade school year, I prayed like there was no tomorrow. I was so thankful when I got a letter telling me who my new teacher was... I'd passed. I shouted, "Thank you Lord!"

CHAPTER 5

Evolving

My eighth and ninth grade school years went pretty well. I started to get serious with my weightlifting and enjoyed drawing. I was introduced to the world of graffiti and tried to learn all I could about it. Several of my schoolmates were drawing graffiti like it was second nature. A few of them called me a "biter" for copying styles. I was just trying to learn the craft. To gain my own style, I incorporated my drawings of comic book characters. Some of my friends said my work was "jake" but I didn't care, it was mine.

Amongst other things, I was still my father's punching bag, which fueled my quest to get stronger. I was also still dealing with Brandon, the neighborhood bully. By the end of ninth grade, we fought about three times. One of the fights came about because he hit my baby brother Brian, who was turning five at the time. It seemed like all of my neighbors were rooting for me during that fight. He was a menace to everybody, and they wanted him to get his just due. The police came and stopped the fight. He wouldn't shut up, so the police arrested him. "This ain't over!" he yelled.

A few days later in school, he wanted to finish where we had left off. At lunch time, we met in the gym locker room. Before I could even drop my book bag, he punched me in the mouth and bounced around in a boxer's stance. "Wassup now?" he blurted.

Something came over me. The taste of my own blood sparked a need to hurt him like never before. I growled as I grabbed him and slammed him into the lockers. I wanted him to remember this ass whippin' with every punch, kick, and wrestling move I unleashed. I was getting a pleasure in ramming him into the lockers. I tried to leave an impression of his head in them. I don't even remember if he threw another punch. After that fight, we never fought again. As a matter of fact, by the tenth grade we were cool.

After three years of being in the concert band and participating in several Memorial Day parades as a bass drummer, I wanted to play football. During the summer before my ninth-grade school year, I went to two-a-days. Because I didn't play for seventh and eighth grade, I was underestimated by the coaches. All they saw was a chubby lad. I worked hard trying to prove myself, but still got nowhere with them. I endured all their verbal abuse... took all the exercises and football routines they threw at me like a champ. I decided to quit when one of them told me that my fat ass would never play.

One of the football coaches had become the school district's athletic director, and he would come to some of my wrestling matches. My highlight was our last bout against Euclid. So far, our team was undefeated, and Euclid gave us a hard time. Some of our star wrestlers lost or barely won their bouts. We were all in a funk. I got myself motivated and started doing push-ups and dips. I bounced around like a boxer before his title match. I was determined to win my match.

Before I went on the mat, my coach pulled me to the side and said, "B.B. I need you to win this! If you win by points, that will give us 3 points... good enough for a tie. GO FOR THE PIN! THAT'S 6 POINTS! GO FOR THE PIN!!!" I went in with determination and so did my opponent. He strutted on the mat chewing gum. The referee made him spit it out. I stared at him with no expression as he taunted me. He thought I was an easy target.

When the ref blew his whistle, we locked up like two grizzly bears. A few minutes seemed like hours. After a while of tussling, my opponent started sneaking jabs to my mouth saying, "Come on nigga... come on nigga!" I pushed him back then lunged at him, slammed him to the ground and pinned him. He didn't know what hit him. My win kept us undefeated.

After the match, the athletic director/football coach came up to me and said, "Hey King, I want you to play ninth grade football for me next year."

I looked at him and said, "No thanks, I'll be in high school!" That felt good. What's funny is he thought I was in the eighth grade. My father went to my wrestling banquet... that really made me feel good.

CHAPTER 6

To Be or Not to Be All I Can Be

High school seemed like smooth sailing. The first few months upon entering the high school, the tenth graders were getting initiated by the seniors. They thought it was fun to beat up on my fellow sophomores, and some went too far and hurt some of them. I refused to be a victim, I vowed to fight back if I got jumped.

I got caught by the seniors during my lunch break. I backed myself into the wall and prepared for battle. As they started throwing blows, I was returning them. I made sure I hit each one of them several times. When it was all over, I was still standing. Some of the seniors began to show me respect. Some of them even took me under their wing.

As far as the homestead, I wasn't getting bothered by my father as much, although he did a lot of complaining. He would look at me and say, "Lifting weights ain't gonna do nothin' for you with all that eatin'!"

I barked, "I'm getting stronger! Look at this muscle!"

He replied, "Aw that ain't shit but hard fat! As long as you keep eatin' the way you do, you'll never be in shape!" I didn't care... I kept lifting anyway.

I didn't know much about weightlifting, so I started buying bodybuilding magazines and followed every plan possible. I wanted my body to look like Lee Haney's, an eight-time Mr. Olympia champion. Lifting weights became more than a form of relieving stress... it became an addiction. Every day I would lift for hours. I would push myself so hard that I went into "Berzerker Mode" (when warriors work themselves into a frenzy before battle). My body would tremble... like I was shivering. My father would try to distract me by telling me if I was to ever stop, I would get very fat... um, yeah.

I remember at fourteen I told him that by the time I turned sixteen, he wouldn't hurt me anymore. He jumped up and roared, "Boy if you ever get the nerve to try me you will end up like Marvin Gaye!"

KONKERER

When I turned sixteen, I was bench pressing over 300 lbs. I remember picking my father up to prove how strong I was. At the time, he weighed around 260 lbs. "Boy, put me down!" he yelled as I carried him up the stairs from the basement. The surprised expression on my mom and dad's face... priceless. When I put him down, he just stared at me in amazement. "Boy, you're too strong for your own good!" he said. My uncle Joe told my mother that I was lifting weights so much so that I could be stronger than my father... he'd figured me out.

Even though my father didn't like that I was lifting so much, he was contributing to it. He worked for the housing projects and would often bring weights home. About three times a week, I would put all the weights on the bar, equaling 250 lbs., and lift until failure. I kept a weekly log of how many times I was able to lift it. I had reached 67 before the hollow metal bar had gotten bent out of shape. I was still able to lift at high school though. By high school graduation, I was benching close to 350. Even though I was very strong, I was still afraid of my father.

During the summer of my eleventh-grade school year, I decided to give football another try. I was dedicated to football conditioning and two-a-days. Even though my hard work earned me a spot starting defensive tackle for junior varsity, I had to deal with favoritism and lack of experience on the varsity squad. Most of the players had older brothers that had paved the way for them. I was upset that tenth graders got chosen before me. It didn't matter, I just wanted to play.

I started every game, except one due to my attitude. I was dealing with some stuff with my father and ended up taking it out on one of my teammates. One of the joys of playing football was that my mother, grandmother and grandfather came to watch me play. My grandfather told me that he was proud of me. My father came to my last game against Parma. He complained because I got kicked out of the game for a penalty. I punched the offensive guard in the helmet for calling me a "nigger." My father didn't care, he was focused on the game. I expected him to attend more games, especially when he told me we shared the same number... "76."

Teenagers believe they have life all figured out, and I was no exception. By my junior year in high school, I had the ultimate plan for my future. Upon graduation, I was going to join the Marines and serve my country for four years, then let them pay for my college education. After college, I would get a high-paying job as an engineer and live happily ever after.

After discussing my so-called future plans with my father, I wasn't so sure what I wanted to do. He barked about how black men had no business in the service.

"But they will pay for my college!" I yelped.

"Bullshit!" he growled. "What if a war breaks out? You'd be one of the first to go and you might get killed. You'll be another nigga fightin' the white man's war! I don't wanna bury a son! Why can't you just go to college? Make me and your mama proud."

He told me a brief story about how he wanted to join the army, but they turned him down because he had flat feet. A few years later, the Vietnam War became a major issue and America was losing. Soldiers, black and white, were getting killed as soon as they touched Vietnam soil. Now the Army was interested in my dad, but he wasn't going to anybody's war. In a year's time he gained over 60 lbs., and the Army wasn't interested anymore. "Gaining that weight saved my life!" he barked proudly. "Boy, go to college! Make somethin' of yourself!"

Since joining the Marines was no longer in my plans, I decided to look into some possible colleges. There were a few schools that really sparked my interest, but I only applied to two; Morris Brown and Bowling Green State University. I favored BGSU more. My cousin Renee was about to graduate from there, and she was making a name for herself. Not only was she an honor student, she fought diligently against racism and became the first black homecoming queen.

I looked up to Renee, and I thought it would be a great honor to follow in her footsteps and make a name for myself. My initial plan was to pursue a degree in engineering and become a walk-on for the football team. I got accepted by the skin of my teeth. I forgot all about Morris Brown and pursued my future with BGSU. My mother had made all the initial preparations to send me off. She constantly warned me not to ruin this opportunity, and I didn't want to let her down.

My senior year in high school didn't go the way I'd planned it. My father had gotten laid off from his job months earlier, and even though he started a successful home renovation company, I felt I had to do something. I decided to forget about football and continue to work at the appliance store. My mother assured me that I didn't have to, but there were things I wanted. You know... like name brand clothes, Jordan's, etc.

Since I had finished all my course requirements for graduation, I decided to take Art and join the choir. Ever since tenth grade, I had tried to take Art, but my guidance counselor wouldn't let me. Instead, she made me take all college prep courses. My art teacher was amazed with my artistic talent and was upset he didn't have time to teach me more.

In choir I sang bass, and would act silly and sing like I was an opera performer. The choir director would often stop the music and ask, "Who's singing like that?" I would look around like I didn't know who it was. After a while she just said, "Whoever is singing like that keep doing it, I love it!" So, I did. She was amazed when she saw me sing in a play. She apologized for cutting me during the choir tryouts when I was in the seventh grade.

I started to get more rebellious against my father. Earlier, we made an agreement that he would pay me for helping him out with the home repairs and landscaping. After the jobs were done, I asked to be paid. He got mad and said, "Nigga I paid you already. You're eating my food!" I told him that he didn't have to worry about me anymore. I stopped helping him.

Several times he asked me for a $100 loan, promising to pay me back. He always paid me back except for the last time. When I asked for my money back he screamed that same phrase again, "You're eating my food dammit! I don't owe you shit!" I couldn't respect him anymore because he wasn't a man of his word.

A few weeks before graduation, my father started acting funny. He started doing things out of the norm. I remember him and his friend trying to convince me to forget about going to college and consider taking up a trade. I honestly couldn't understand why, especially after that sob story about why he didn't want me to go to the Marines. In my own way, I told both of them to go to hell. College was my ticket to freedom.

CHAPTER 7

Future Crushed

Graduation went smoothly. I felt like I was sitting on top of the world. That sensation only lasted a week. On Father's Day, my father started tripping big time. I said, "Hey Dad Happy Father's Day!" He looked at me like he wanted to kill me.

He barked, "Nigga don't say shit to me!" I granted him his wish. I wanted to spend some quality time with him, but I ended up spending that time with my girlfriend's father instead.

When I got home that evening, my father was sitting at the kitchen table. "You can't speak nigga?!" he barked.

"You told me not to talk to you!" I barked back.

He jumped up and yelled, "Who the hell you think you talkin' to? I'll kill you nigga!!!" Even though I didn't respond, I wasn't going to back down. "Get that piece of shit out of my driveway!" he said, referring to my '77 Buick Regal. It was just sitting there on account that it needed a starter. I pushed it out onto the street, hoping that it wouldn't get a ticket overnight. "If you don't like it, get the fuck out!" he said. While I was trying to call my uncle Gary he yelled, "Get the fuck off my phone! If you don't like it, get the fuck out!"

The next morning I tried calling my uncle, but he was at work so I left him a message. He didn't call back until that afternoon. It turned out great for me because he said I could stay with him until I left for college. It was too late for my car... my father had me call a junkyard to come and pick it up. I didn't know what to do or who to call. I just signed over the title and accepted the measly $35 they offered. I hated him for that.

The summer went pretty cool. While staying with my uncle, I was working part-time at Sohio car wash on Northfield, and best of all I was away from my father. I spent as much quality time with my girlfriend as possible because she really didn't want me to leave.

KONKERER

It was rumored that my dad was seen at the park being "up close and personal" with another woman. I really didn't take it seriously until my uncle caught him in the act. I remember him busting through the door yelling, "Your father is cheatin' on my sister! I just saw that fat muthafucka kissin' some fat bitch at Woodhill Park! Let's go get your mother outta that house!" I was ready.

As soon as we got to my mom's house, uncle Gary wasted no time telling her what he saw. You could tell that she was hurting, but she just smiled and said, "God is going to handle it." Uncle Gary was furious. He couldn't understand why she wouldn't leave. I believed she was doing what was best at the time, going with the flow. I tried not to worry too much about her that summer. I knew she could handle herself.

My mother had rented a car so she and my uncle could drive me to school. During the two-hour ride, all I could think of was working to the best of my ability and making my mother proud of me. When we got there, my uncle and I unloaded the car and went to my assigned room. I was the first person to a room I shared with four other people. I was also the only black person in the room.

After my mother and uncle left, I unpacked my things and waited for my roommates. Upon their arrival, I introduced myself. Two of them were from Canton and the other two were from Willowick. You could tell that they weren't around black people because they started asking me stupid "Black" questions like, "Do Black people tan?"

I told them to wait until Christmas and figure out the answer themselves. We sat around and talked for about an hour, then went to get something to eat.

After a month, the racist questions started going too far, and they started doing stupid things like soiling my bed with baby powder and lotion. I already had a short temper and was ready to fight somebody. I would block the door and refuse to let anyone leave until they cleaned up the messes they made. Before I left home, my father warned me about the stupid, racist stuff they could do. Even though we weren't getting along, I took heed to his warning.

In order to keep my composure, I read a Bible that my grandmother gave me, and listened to the Winans and Take 6. Two of my roommates hated when I played my music. They knew I was mad about all the stupid things they did. One day after class, I came to the dorm room and noticed one of my cassette tapes was destroyed. That, along with some other stupid stuff they did, set my temper off and I "hulked out." I ended up fighting two of them. I was in so much of a rage that I couldn't control myself... it sort of scared me because I reminded myself of my father.

After the fight, my roommates had a meeting with the RA stating that it was unsafe to be around me. Little did they know, I had already approached the RA and guidance counselor about the things they did. To make living uneasy, they nitpicked and complained about anything, including allowing my friends and line brothers in the room.

KONKERER

One day while I was washing laundry, I was approached by an upperclassman (who also happened to be white). He told me that I shouldn't fight unless I really had to. "You are filled with a lot of anger and hate. Don't let it consume you, you have nothing to prove" he said. He was a martial arts student who believed that one should fight only in self-defense. He let me borrow three booklets to read and to this day, I couldn't remember the names of those books if you paid me.

What I do remember is that each book focused on Zen, which is a form of meditation and insight. Buddhists practice Zen as a form of living peacefully. I also learned not to get angry so easily and to be humble. I'm still trying to utilize these values successfully. The only downfall of learning to be "Zen-like" is that I'm often perceived as being SOFT.

Academically, I was performing below average, especially in Sociology. My professor wouldn't help me with the course either. He would just tell me to read the book. I did what he told me, but the test questions were different from what I read in the book and his lectures. My mother told me to find a tutor, but there wasn't one for the class.

Along with my roommates, there were several other events that affected my studies. My aunt Georgia and Mr. Bonner (my good friend's grandfather and mentor) had passed away. My girlfriend was also stressing me out. I decided to go home for a weekend to get some needed mental rest and attend my girlfriend's homecoming.

When I got home, I found out that we had won an award for being "Family of the Year" by Westwood Elementary School's PTA, where my baby brother and sister attended. My mother didn't want the award. She felt it was a farce. We weren't "family of the year" material, but you would never know from the outside looking in.

One of my courses was in weight conditioning. After a month in the class, my teacher was amazed at how strong I was and urged me to join the weightlifting team. Not only did they train me to lift properly, they were looking for someone to replace the senior who was graduating in May.

I was making so much progress that I amazed myself. One of the coaches set a goal for me to be able to lift a total weight of 1,625 lbs. (bench presses 450 lbs., squats 550 lbs. and dead lifts 625 lbs.) by the end of the semester. I thought that would be impossible, but I pushed myself to the limit. My father was my motivation. By the end of the semester I reached a total weight of 1,780 lbs., (bench presses 500 lbs., squats 600 lbs. and dead lifts 680 lbs.), more than my initial goal.

I thought my college life was making a turn for the better. My talents started to speak for me. Because of some of the artwork I had done with an Art major, my professor sought me out and urged me to change my major from Engineering to Art. To think that I could possibly get scholarships for both weightlifting and art uplifted my spirits. Not only would I have excelled in the

Art coursework, I would've been doing something I loved. Things seemed to work out smoothly until life threw another curve ball.

During the school break, I received a letter in the mail from college saying that I was put on academic probation, which included being suspended for one semester. My whole world was crushed. My mom was so upset with me that if she could have killed me and gotten away with it, she would have. Hell, her look of disgust alone made me want to just crawl up under a rock and die. I tried to do all I could to regain her trust.

I had to make the most of this time off, so I got a job to save money for the next semester. A few weeks later, the college sent a refund check. My father asked me to sign it, and I was thinking he was going to put the money back into my college account for the next semester. A few days later, my mom told me that the money was not there. When he got home from work, I asked him if he was going to put the money back in the account and he barked back, "Hell nawl! You flunked out nigga! You ain't goin' back... not wit my fuckin' money!"

I wanted to kill him. I wasn't going to let him get the best of me. I was going to keep working until I got enough money to send myself back to college and work hard to stay there.

CHAPTER 8

I Want to Go Away

I started to get depressed, and there was nothing I wanted more than to just get away. I told my girlfriend that I was moving to Bowling Green, Ohio and wanted her to go with me... start fresh. She didn't want to. A friend of mine told me that she was cheating on me with a white guy, but I didn't believe him. Even though our relationship was rocky, I still believed she loved me.

A few months went by and I didn't make it to college. I didn't care, and it showed. My parents' relationship was getting worse, and they were both taking their anger out on me. My girlfriend kept telling me that I was gaining weight and she wanted me to start lifting weights again. She was losing her attraction to my appearance, but I didn't notice... maybe I didn't care.

A few weeks before Thanksgiving, my mother couldn't put up with my dad's crap anymore so she left him. A week later, my girlfriend and I broke up. Even though we were apart, I would give her occasional rides home from work. All of a sudden, I became a stalker. I found myself driving past her house in hopes of getting a glimpse of her.

One day I drove past the house and saw her mother in the driveway. I stopped to speak. Her mother told me that she had moved to the west side, but she didn't know where. She also said that she was pregnant. I spent months wondering, hoping she was having my baby. My mom believed that she wasn't. A year later, I found out her baby was half white. My heart dropped.

I sat in the backyard by the tree and burst into tears. My father looked out the window and came outside. Hoping to get some sort of sympathy, I gave him a hug. He paused for a second and said, "I hope you ain't cryin' bout that little bitch!" He reached into his pocket and pulled out some condoms and said, "Here, now go find you some other bitches to fuck!" As he walked back in the house I started to cry harder. My life was in shambles and I didn't know what to do.

KONKERER

Full of depression, life didn't seem to matter at all. I didn't care about anything, not even my weight or hygiene. My family didn't hesitate to let me know either. "Bobby, you stink... go take a shower!" I must've been having a mental breakdown or something. No matter how bad they talked about me, I didn't seem to care.

I was constantly having thoughts of suicide. I remember sitting in the backyard staring at a big tree by the woods, wondering how my family would feel if they were to find me hanging there. "They probably wouldn't care" I thought. A few days later, I got into an argument with my brother in front of our friends. He kept poking fun at me about how bad I smelled.

"You ain't nothin' but a bum!" he shouted. As they laughed, I realized that I was nothing more to my family and friends than just an embarrassment.

The next day I waited until everyone left the house, went into the garage and found a rope. I took the rope to the backyard and sat near a big tree. I started making a noose to wrap around my neck. When I finished I just sat there, periodically looking up at the tree as if it would be a voice of reason. I was looking for an excuse not to hang myself.

There was an old dog house sitting near the tree. I stood on top of it to tie the rope around a large branch. Both the tree and the dog house were located near a small hill. I'd say it was about ten to thirteen feet deep. While standing on the dog house, I put the noose around my neck, closed my eyes and thought to myself, "So long cruel world." I took a step into the darkness... or so I thought.

I opened my eyes to find that I was just hanging there. I really didn't feel any pain... just a slight tug around my neck. The crazy thing was that I was still breathing. "Dammit!" I yelled. Either I didn't make the noose right, or my neck was too strong from all those neck exercises in high school wrestling and weightlifting. As I hung there, I was debating if I should cut the rope. Before I could react, I heard a cracking noise. After a minute or two of silence, the tree branch snapped. The branch, the rope and I tumbled down the hill.

As I lay on the ground I thought to myself, "I hope no one saw this." I didn't move for a good thirty minutes... I just cried. It was bad enough that I felt like a failure; I couldn't even kill myself right. I sat up and prayed for forgiveness. I took the noose from around my neck and trudged up the hill. I sat on the dog house and stared into the woods. I made a vow that I was going to live my life to the fullest, and no matter how bad my life got, I would never try to commit suicide again.

My mother, siblings and I lived on Walford for about a year and a half. During that time, I was looking for a job. My mother gave me the deadline of June 1st by which to do so. While I was searching for jobs, I would go spend time with my grandfather. Due to his illness, he had moved in with my aunt. He was a short, skinny man but he was powerful and well respected. Hell, even my dad had a lot of respect for him. My grandfather was a war veteran and A REAL AMERICAN HERO... at least to ME.

Spending time with my grandfather started to bring a sense of HOPE to my life. He would smile at me and say, "You're young Bobby. Go out and have fun... LIVE!" I really didn't want to. I'd found some form of salvation being with him and listening to his many life stories.

I remember when the Gulf War started my grandfather, a devoted Republican, got so excited. The politician in him believed what Bush was doing was right. "Don't you wanna go serve your country Bobby?" he asked me with a big smile on his face. I looked at him like he was crazy. I wasn't going to war for anybody! I had gained a lot of weight because of my depression, so I knew I had no chance of going anyway.

When my grandfather passed, I felt kind of betrayed. He was my mentor, and he was the only person that seemed to make things right at that time. He taught me strength beyond the physical. A strength that made me realize that I would be okay, and that I could not let life get the best of me.

June was soon approaching, and I still hadn't found a job. One evening, I was sitting on the stoop of our apartment while talking to my neighbor about a possible job. We could hear my aunt, who lived across the way, yelling at my two cousins because they wouldn't finish their homework. All of a sudden we heard her scream, "Forget about it then. Don't do your homework and grow up to be a bum like Bobby!" Afterwards, there was an eerie moment of silence.

My neighbor just shook his head in disbelief. I wanted to go over there and curse her out, but I couldn't move. As the tears flowed down my cheeks, my neighbor gave me a pat on my back and told me that some people don't mean any harm with what they say; sometimes it's the only way to show they care. I thought to myself, "If that's their way of showing how much they care, then I don't want anybody to give a damn about me."

After my mother and father sold the house, my father decided to get an apartment on Walford also. My father let me drive his truck because he didn't have a place to put it. I was surprised he let me use it. Back then, trucks weren't allowed to be outside overnight. One of my neighbors found a vacant garage for me to park the truck in.

I found a job working for the Department of Transportation for the summer. I was hoping to get hired full-time. Remembering my mother's warning, I told her that I didn't start until June 6th. "I said the first!" she yelled. I think she didn't believe me. On the evening of the 1st, she kicked me out and my father let me stay over for the night. The next morning, I found my uncle and stayed with him until the day I started working.

During the summer, I got into a car accident with a white guy in a Volvo. Though he sped out in front of me, I was deemed "at fault" by North Randall police. I called my father back to back while at the police station... no answer. We exchanged information and went on our way. Two hours later, I finally found my father and told him what happened. "Why didn't you call me?!" he barked. I just shook my head.

I didn't get the full-time job at the Department of Transportation, so I enrolled at Tri-C for Commercial Art. I had enough money to buy art supplies and other necessities. When I told my father I was in school, he yelled at me claiming there was no money in Commercial Art, that a guy he worked with had a degree in it but couldn't find work. I did really well in my classes, but I couldn't get financial aid. After a few months with no work, my mother kicked me out again. I slept in the truck for a few days until I found my uncle. He let me stay with him. He also wanted me to find a job.

While driving my uncle's car, I got pulled over in Maple Heights because his license plate was bent. I got arrested for a suspended license. The suspension was due to failing to show proof of insurance during an accident I was involved in six months earlier. At the court hearing I was fined over $800. Since I couldn't pay right then, I had to serve time in jail. Each day in jail equaled $30, and I was let go after five days because the police felt their space was needed for harsher criminals.

King

Upon release, I signed an agreement to have the remainder of the fine paid within 90 days. I didn't bother to pay until I was twenty-six. While paying the fine, the clerk (who was a senior citizen) said something that stuck with me. "You know young man, sparrows are free... be like a sparrow, be free." I now use that phrase every time I mentor troubled youth.

There was a blind guy that my uncle and I were affiliated with who wanted to buy my father's truck. The funny thing was that his last name was also King. My father agreed to sell the truck. My uncle Gary agreed to pay for the truck for all the things Mr. King had done for him. I called my father and told him to come by Mr. King's house after 2:00 p.m., when uncle Gary got home from work. I explained to him that uncle Gary was paying for the truck.

My father arrived an hour early. I asked him why he came so early, but he ignored me and started talking to Mr. King. My father signed over the title and gave it to him. As Mr. King walked away, my father called out to him and asked, "Hey when are you going to pay me?"

Mr. King turned around and said, "That's between you and Gary." My father looked at me and went off... calling me every fat dummy name possible. I argued back, and soon we were about to fight. Obviously, he didn't pay attention to me when I told him uncle Gary was paying for the truck.

KONKERER

While we were arguing, Mr. King came out and called us into his house where we continued the argument. My father tried to over-talk me and yelled out, "He's the reason why me and my wife ain't together now!"

I growled back, "You are a damn liar! You know why my mama left you! Tell the truth!"

My father tried to strike me yelling, "You ain't gon disrespect me! You ain't gon disrespect me!"

Mr. King yelled for us to calm down and explained the agreement he and uncle Gary had. A few minutes later, uncle Gary came and gave him the money. Later that night, I had a conversation with Mr. King and he told me no matter how bad my father treated me, I should always treat him with respect. I told him that it's also wrong for parents to provoke their children. "Indeed" Mr. King said while nodding his head.

CHAPTER 9

Welcome to E.C.

After my brother Stef graduated from Warrensville, my mother decided to move back to the house in East Cleveland. I spent a whole month preparing the place for my mother. Since it was a two-family unit, my mother let my brother and me rent the lower half. It was our own bachelor pad.

Moving back to East Cleveland seemed to be okay. About a week after we moved in, a new reality hit me.

While getting off the bus after a long day of looking for a job, I saw a huge crowd gathered around the corner store. When I reached the crowd, I saw a teenage girl lying lifeless against the building in a pool of her own blood. She was shot in the shoulder and bled to death due to a drive-by.

I was furious. The crowd acted like it was nothing... just another day in E.C. As the paramedics carried the girl away, one of the store employees brought out a bucket of bleach water and a push broom. I just stood there and stared as her diluted blood streamed down the sidewalk and into the sewer. I thought to myself, "Welcome to East Cleveland... this sure isn't Warrensville."

Around that time, I didn't have much of a relationship with my father. I asked him to help me get a position at his job and he refused. He claimed that I wouldn't be able to fit the company's uniforms. A year later he helped my brother get a job there, and to be honest, that wasn't what he wanted. He wanted my father to help him pay for barber school. That was a kick in the teeth.

I remember when I was twenty-two my brother and uncle had a disagreement about a car. We all met up at my uncle's house to resolve the situation. My father came as some sort of mediator. After hearing that I had fixed the master cylinder on the car, he lost focus and started questioning me.

"Wait a minute, why the hell did you fix the car? You don't know anything about cars!" he barked.

KONKERER

"I do know about cars!" I snapped back. We ended up arguing, and he stood up and headed for me. I stood up, ready to fight. My uncle ran and stood in front of him. That's when I noticed the knife in my father's hand. I realized that he was ready to kill me, and if I hadn't noticed the knife, he probably would've been successful.

As my uncle calmed us down, I didn't care about anything else but going home, and for the life of me I can't tell you why I let my father take me. My uncle thought I had some kind of mental illness... like battered dog syndrome. Maybe I did. After dropping me off, my father left then came back over later that night so we could talk.

With my eyes full of tears, I asked him why he hated me so much. "I don't hate you at all, I love you very much Bobby" he answered. After a moment of silence, he took a deep breath and said, "Your mother is a very strong woman. When I called her names, she'd laugh. When I knocked her upside the head, she fought back. When I hurt you, she'd break down and cry. I realized that hurting you was the only way I could get to her." I already hated him, and telling me this made the hate grow even more. All I could think about was the times that he would beat me to a pulp for no reason. After that night, I stopped talking to him.

I became somewhat of a hermit. I went out when I had to; you know, like going to the store, to work, to visit my family, etc. It seemed that every time I opened up to the world, I was exposed to something crazy. I almost got robbed by a crackhead for my bus fare, I kept running into women who wanted nothing but to use me, and I was morbidly obese. Everyone looked at me like I was a freak of nature. I felt like if this was what life had to offer, I'd rather stay in the house.

A few months after my twenty fourth birthday, I got into an argument with my brother Stef about being cooped up in the house. "Bobby, you're young. You need to go out and have fun!" he yelled. I really didn't want to hear what he had to say, but in the back of my mind I knew he was right.

I decided to go out and get a taste of the night life. I started hanging out at a local bar around the corner. There, I was able to meet some very interesting people; drug dealers, crackheads, drunks, and whores in particular. Watching them struggle gave me the incentive to go back to school. I remembered the vow I'd made to myself to get my degree and make my mom proud. I even did my school work at the bar... yes, I did.

At the bar, I had many conversations with the "people of the night" as my mom would call them. They would share their life stories with me, then ask me how or why I let myself get so big. I wanted to tell them to shut the hell up. But I didn't; I just listened. I guess God wanted me to listen.

I had come to the conclusion that they too had been abused in some way, and crack or alcohol helped them cope with life. The streets became their sense of security, and venting to me gave them a sense of clarity. These people helped mold my outlook on life... either you're living or just existing.

I found a job working for Michael's Arts & Crafts. One of the managers was very leery in hiring me and stayed on my back every chance he got. I didn't pay him any attention, I just kept doing my job. One manager that liked me wanted me to utilize my talents by drawing and doing other crafts for the store. I also helped out in the framing department. Working at Michael's seemed promising.

After my probation period, two of the store managers called me to the office and told me that after their meeting, they'd come to the conclusion that I was no longer needed. It was obvious why they let me go... it was because I was fat and black. They also let me go on the day the manager who liked me was off. I called to get my W-2 statement at the end of the year. Both the managers that let me go were no longer there, and the remaining one asked me, "What happened? Why did you quit?" I looked at him in confusion and told him that I didn't quit, that I was let go by the other two managers. He apologized and asked me to reapply. I decided not to.

As the years passed, the "people of the night" became somewhat of an extended family. They showed me a lot of love and respect, and even if it was fake... so what?! I was getting the comfort that I'd longed for. My mother couldn't understand it. She'd always ask sarcastic questions like, "Where are you going? TO THE BAR?!?" I didn't care, at least there I felt appreciated. It was my ghetto Cheers.

King

I started going to the bar early, like around 8 p.m., just to sit and think or find my own form of clarity. Usually by 11 p.m. I was surrounded by people from the neighborhood. I felt like a King. It seemed like every person that entered the bar made their way to me to just shake my hand or to buy me a drink. I hardly ever bought a drink. There were a few people trying to figure me out.

"Hey, what do you do?" they'd ask. "Nothing" I'd respond.

There were several times when a drunk or crackhead walked up to me to say that I seemed out of place... like I didn't belong there. I remember one saying, "You look like an angel sitting in the midst of demons!" That freaked me out.

All good things don't last for long. In the wink of an eye, I watched my circle fade. If they weren't getting high off wet, they were snitching and robbing each other. I started to lose respect for some of them. I grew weary of the ones I'd once found comfort in. I saw no growth. I got tired of seeing some of them take round trips in and out of jail, and I got fed up with hearing the sound of gunshots. They were as common as SUVs driving by with booming systems. I decided to make changes in my life, but I couldn't seem to get away from the night life. I was still addicted.

To pass time, I started reading comic books again. I was often asked about my fascination with the Incredible

Hulk. Most believe it's the raging maniac that he erupts into. Well, that's not necessarily true. You see, even though he's just a comic book character, we have a lot in common. Our first name is Robert, we're from Ohio, we both have a thirst for knowledge, we both had abusive fathers and we both learned how to suppress the anger within. To be honest, we're both afraid of what that anger could cause.

When I was in my late teens I didn't follow the Incredible Hulk comics much, but I noticed that he had transformed into a grey-skinned, sarcastic, suit-wearing brute. He worked in Las Vegas as a bodyguard/hitman under the name of "Joe Fixit." At first, I really wasn't feeling that version of the Hulk, but I liked how he wasn't portrayed as a mindless brute screaming "HULK SMASH!"

By the time my brother graduated from high school in '92, the Green Hulk, the Grey Hulk and Bruce Banner had merged together to form "The Professor". This Hulk possessed the size, strength and green skin just like the Green Hulk, but he had the looks and genius of Bruce Banner. I really liked this version of the Hulk. He possessed a Zen-like manner and only lost his temper when he was fully provoked.

This Hulk displayed his emotional side and his fears of losing his Zen to become evil. I really identified with this version. As I got older, I had fears that I would end up being a loose cannon like my father was. At one time, I hated looking in the mirror because I started looking more like him. Maybe it's the reason why I don't wear a mustache. I still see him in the mirror, but now I accept it wholeheartedly.

It seemed like my weight had increased significantly as each year went by, and it didn't go unnoticed. Some of my family members swore that I was trying to eat myself into an early grave. Sure, I loved food like the next fat guy, but that wasn't the case. I really didn't know why I was gaining weight like that. I can still hear my father's voice blaming my many years of weightlifting. To be honest, if it weren't for weightlifting, I wouldn't have been able to take care of myself or even move around when I was 700 lbs.

Can you imagine going over to your family members' house only to hear them clown you for sitting on their furniture? Once, I went over to an aunt's house whose couch was already broken by her own kids. I sat on that couch and found out later that she complained. There was another time when I attended a family get together at another aunt's house. She had an oversized recliner that was built for very large people. I know this because I was going to buy the same chair. As soon as I sat in the chair, she told me not to sit on it, claiming I had already broken the leg off her ottoman I once sat on in her living room.

I told her that I didn't break it, but she didn't believe me. I later found out that my baby brother had broken it by jumping off the landing. I told her, and my brother even admitted to it, but she still didn't believe us. From then on, I made a promise to myself that if I was to ever go back to another family member's house, I would only sit on either the stairs or the floor. If they had a problem with that, I would never go back.

After my twenty-fifth birthday, I enrolled into Bryant & Stratton College for an Associate degree in Computer Drafting. I was finally eligible for financial aid, and I was ready to roll. I moved into an apartment downtown in Reserve Square just to be close to the school. I got work study with a pizza shop near the school. I felt a sense of pride because things started going the right way. After my second semester my grade point average dropped a few points, and my counselor took me off work study. I was so mad at her. I could see if I wasn't doing well... but I was still on the Dean's List.

There was a gym in the complex, so I decided to start up a workout routine. I figured if I was going to be big, I might as well be in shape. I worked out twice a day, doing cardio or running in the swimming pool in the morning and lifting weights in the evening. It seemed like no matter how hard I worked, I didn't lose any weight; I just got stronger and more agile. I also played football on the weekends.

I met a man that worked out at the gym. He told me that the Crazy Horse Saloon was hiring for bouncers, and that I should apply and use him as a reference. I had nothing to lose, so I gave it a try. I got the job as soon as I applied. I had to wear a black suit and bowtie, but I couldn't find a suit jacket my size. They allowed me to wear a black vest. It felt odd doing security looking like a penguin, but I was blessed to have a job.

I was wet behind the ears, and along with having a short temper, I was considered dangerous for the company. One of the bouncers took me under his wing. He told me that security was ninety percent mental and ten percent physical. I would watch how he worked. He was so mild-mannered, but he was a very good fighter. The two years I worked there, I gained a lot of knowledge from him.

In 1998, I graduated from Bryant & Stratton with flying colors. I was upset with my father because he didn't come to my graduation. It didn't matter because we had just started talking again. My mother and grandmother attended the ceremony... that was good enough for me.

The speaker of the ceremony was Ronnie Duncan, the sportscaster for WOIO-TV Channel 19 News. I met him at the gym in Reserve Square. We became cool and I loved talking to him. He motivated me in everything I did. After the graduation ceremony, he asked me if I was going to keep going and pursue my Bachelor's degree. "Most definitely!" I replied.

I knew I was going to get a good job as an architectural draftsman. The school's job placement director had several interviews lined up for me. After three interviews, I noticed the same pattern. They would all take me to the second or third floor by stairs, then after the interview was over, send me downstairs via elevator. They knew they weren't going to hire me as soon as they saw me. They just went through with the routine instead of honestly saying, "Hey Mr. King, you're too overweight and a high risk for us."

CHAPTER 10
Living… or Existing

The job search process was getting very tedious. I started to feel like a failure all over again, but I kept pushing. My grandmother's health started failing, so my mom and a few of her siblings decided it was best for her to move into our house. At the time, it seemed like our house got turned upside down. My brother and I were staying on the first floor, but when my grandmother moved in my brother moved into the attic, and I to the basement. I must admit that it was a bit uncomfortable, and it seemed like our house had revolving doors because family and nurses were constantly running in and out the house.

After a few weeks the family stopped coming around as often; leaving me, along with my mom and my other two siblings, the burden of taking care of Grandma. It was more than a humbling experience having to care for her in EVERY way. She was taking a prescription drug that would cause her to become immobile, similar to paralysis. Even though she wasn't a big woman, it seemed like her weight had doubled. Carrying her often left me with constant back pain.

After a while, taking care of Grandma started to become more and more emotional for us, especially for my mother. There were several times when she would just break down into tears, and because she was a diabetic, her levels would often get out of control. One day, she called home and told me to call one of my aunts and ask her to come over and help out for a few hours. My mom decided to rest at the hospital until her levels were lowered. My sister and I didn't worry because she'd done this many times before.

Within minutes, several of my mother's siblings came over, all in an uproar. They were constantly drilling us over our mother's whereabouts. I must admit that I was being difficult, but what else could you expect? The responsibility of taking care of my grandmother was thrown into our laps. I can only imagine how emotional it was for my younger siblings, who were seventeen at the time.

KONKERER

On my twenty eighth birthday I wanted to spend some time alone and decided to go to the bar. My mother got very upset and gave me grief about it. Our emotions got the best of us and we ended up arguing. When I got to the bar, I just sat there. The barmaid came up to me and asked for my order. I ordered four shots of Paul Masson and a beer. "It's my birthday!" I shouted as she stared at me. She brought me an oversized wine glass filled with brandy along with my beer.

The barmaid added several more shots and said, "Happy Birthday Big Baby!" (a nickname the old heads at the bar called me). After a few sips of brandy, I started to shed a few tears.

Two weeks after my birthday, my mother took my grandmother to see her doctor. An aunt and uncle came over to our house a few hours later to see how Grandma was doing. My mother called the house soon after. After talking to my mother, my aunt slammed the phone down, then started cursing at us and kicking our furniture around. "Momma has to stay in a hospice now because they don't want to take care of her anymore! Fuck y'all!" she yelled. My sister and I froze with "what the hell" expressions on our faces. Before I could fully react to her outburst, my uncle grabbed her and carried her out of the house. Can you believe that?

Later that day, my sister and I went to see how Grandma was doing. There were a few of my aunts present. My anger was getting the best of me and I didn't talk to any of them, I just kept my focus on my grandmother. I could tell she had taken that medicine again because she just lay there in a comatose state.

While I was staring at her, I was wondering what she was thinking. I was wondering if she was ready to go home. I didn't want her to die, but I didn't want to see her suffer anymore. I kept thinking about all the promises she made me keep (sharing all my God-given talents with the world... i.e. singing, art, writing, etc.). As my mind wandered, Grandma looked at me, smiled and mumbled, "Hey baby" then went back into her comatose trance. It seemed like she was letting me know that I didn't have to worry anymore. I got up, kissed her on the forehead and went into the waiting room to talk to my sister and cousins. Grandma went home a few days later.

During the funeral, I sat all the way in the back. I was still upset with some of my aunts and uncles for leaving us to care for Grandma as they carried on with their lives. I stared with no emotion as they cried like lost puppies. As the casket closed, the cries got louder. While briefly looking at my uncle Gary, my aunt Julie and my mother, I felt a tear roll down my cheek. I couldn't imagine losing any of them, especially in the lowly state I was in back then. It seemed like they always knew what to say to keep me going. They kept me inspired.

After Grandma's passing, I went back in search of employment. My brother told me that his job at Cablevision was hiring, but I had to apply through a temp agency. I got the job and went through two weeks of training. After the training, I started work. My spirits were uplifted again. During my first day of work, the girl in HR suggested that I work at the department on East 30th. I told her "No thanks, I'd rather stay here." The department at Severance Towne Center was close to my house. I didn't realize that she was giving me the heads up about what went on there. Yes, my weight was a factor.

After a week, the day manager stared at me and sent me to HR. The girl in HR told me that the manager didn't want me to work for her. I asked why but she wouldn't answer. On my way home, I sat at the bus stop and cried. I felt like I had let my brother down. When I got home, I called the girl in HR and asked her why I was let go. She told me that she had been trying to give me hints about what went on there, but I hadn't caught on.

I started to feel depressed again until my uncle's friend asked me to do some odd jobs for him. After doing several home repairs, I decided to carry on my father's home renovation business. This was the first time my father seemed proud of me. He even gave me some old tools and let me work on his license and bond. I was finally doing something I liked, and it wasn't like I didn't know what I was doing; I learned from the best. I also designed floor plans, wrote resumes for people, created business cards and letterheads. Thus, my home renovation/graphic business was born. I called it "King Jr. Inc."

The home renovation business only lasted until 1999, a few months after my baby brother and sister graduated from high school. I didn't care because I started to focus on other things. I also started to hang at the bar more often. On the lighter nights, I would sit and draw all night. I helped out with security whenever they needed me to and sold weed to supplement my income. I wasn't trying to get rich with it, just needed money to get by. I gave up on looking for employment because I got tired of being treated like a freak of nature.

Around this time, I was fed up and done with my father, especially after what he did to my mother. He tried to sell the two-family house without my mother's knowledge. When I called him about it, he caught a major attitude.

"Hell yeah I'm selling that damn house! Ya'll ain't doin' shit with it!"

He told my mother that she could buy him out and referred an appraiser. I was so upset that the house was over-appraised, and my father got a good amount of money. My mother was distraught because that money could've helped her with repairs to the house. After I approached him about the situation, he acted as if it wasn't his problem.

CHAPTER 11
Oh the Pain

A few months before my first niece was born, I started having sharp chest pains. I'd had them before when I was eighteen. After an EKG test, the doctor told me that the cause of the pain came from chest muscle inflammation. "It's common with people who constantly lift heavy weights" he said.

By the time my niece was born, the pain got sharper and I started losing my breath. "I'm not going to make it to see my 30th birthday" I thought. My morbid obesity contributed to my condition, and I blamed myself for so big. I didn't let it stop me; I had registered to go back to school for my Bachelor's degree in the fall, and I was still going to the bar.

The night of my 30th birthday was so special to me. I didn't go to the bar. I stayed home and celebrated with my brother Brian, my sister Jaqui and Marie, my niece's mother. They bought liquor and food and we just sat around drinking and talking. "I made it!" I thought as I sat on the floor in front of the heater vent.

I started classes a week later. I remember going to school extra early, so I could take my time getting to my classroom. I had to make several stops while walking down the long corridor, so I could catch my breath. By the time I made it to my seat, I felt like I was going to pass out from exhaustion.

A few weeks later, I was approached by an older man while sitting in the lobby of my school. "Hey son, how are you?" he asked. "I'm okay, you?" I replied. He paused for a moment, then sat down next to me. He asked me if I was happy with my life. It was obvious that he was talking about my weight problem, so I told him no. He then asked me if I had been eating sugar. I told him yes. This was getting kind of scary because I was literally eating sugar by the spoonful. Don't ask me why.

"I want you to stop that!" he yelled and put his hand on my head and started to pray. When he finished he walked away saying, "We have plans for you son. Oh yes, big plans!" I shrugged him off thinking he was crazy. I never saw him again.

I told my mother about the encounter with the older man and she said he could've been an angel. "He couldn't have been" I thought to myself. I was in doubt because I was often approached by random people claiming that they cared about my well-being. They never tried to help me find possible solutions to my weight problem, they were just annoyances.

A few weeks after that encounter, my health started getting worse. It was a Friday night and I was getting ready to go to the bar. After taking a shower and getting dressed, my chest felt like it was about to explode, and I could barely walk. My mother told me to call 911. I refused because I didn't want the paramedics to treat me like garbage. My mother asked me several times what I was going to do. Out of stubbornness, I wouldn't respond. She threw her hands up in the air and walked into her bedroom.

I just sat in the living room thinking to myself that I was going to die. An hour later, my friend came by to see why I hadn't made it to the bar yet. When she noticed that I didn't look well, she called my sister. My sister was about to leave with her best friend but decided to stick around for a few minutes to see if I was okay. They both spent what seemed to be hours trying to convince me to go to the hospital. I was going to stand my ground, but the pain was so unbearable that I gave in.

When the paramedics came, they were trying to figure out how to get me into the ambulance. It seemed that they didn't care that I was in pain. They made me walk down the stairs to the ambulance. Their first mistake was trying to squeeze my big butt through the tiny side door. "This is not working!" I screamed as they all forcefully pushed. They were determined to make me fit in.

Since trying to squeeze me into the side door didn't work, they walked me to the back of the ambulance and told me to sit on the floor while they pushed and pulled me in. I don't think they realized that there was a rail on the floor. As they pulled me in, the rail started digging further into the side of my butt. "You're hurting me!" I yelled.

"Mr. King you are a very, very large man. We are doing the best we can!" one of the medics yelped.

After finally getting situated in the ambulance, one of the medics grabbed my right arm and started looking for a vein. "You're not going to find a vein there, use my hand" I said.

"I got it!" he snarled.

After several minutes of him ravaging through my arm pit with a needle, I yelled "Dammit... that hurts! I told you that you're not going to find a vein there, use my hand!"

He yelled back, "And I said I got it!"

After a few more minutes of no success, I grabbed him and growled, "MY HAND!!!"

"Okay" he mumbled. I swore he called me "fat ass" under his breath.

When we reached the hospital, one of the medics came up to me and said, "Okay Mr. King, what I want you to do is stand up, turn around and fall back onto the gurney... it's the only way." Can you believe those bastards wanted me to take a Nestea plunge? I refused to just fall back like that, so I just sat down on the gurney. As the medics got me situated, they rolled me off while staring at me like I was some kind of sideshow freak. On the way to the ER, I heard people whispering. "He should be ashamed of himself!" someone blurted out. I just kept my eyes closed until they took me to a room.

The nurses either just stared or hissed as they prepped me for several tests. One of the nurses cut my pants off in order to insert a catheter. They were having difficulty getting it in. I told them I could get up and use the bathroom on my own. I wasn't trying to give them a hard time, but they were treating me like garbage and constantly leaving the room while I was exposed to the world. One nurse came into the room and laid a sheet over me. I thanked her as she walked out. She turned around and just smiled at me. I started to feel at ease and dozed off, only to be awakened by the nurses successfully ramming the catheter into my member. I yelled at them as I lay there in pain.

I started to have ill thoughts. That night, I just lay there and cried. I tried praying, but all I could say was "Lord, I'm not ready to die." My stay there seemed so lonely, even though my family came to visit. I started to get aggravated by all the nurses who either came in to poke me with needles, give me meds, breathing treatments, or just to take a look. Like I said... I was treated like a sideshow freak.

The next day, two physical therapists came in to have me step on a scale. I almost passed out when I found out that I weighed 692 lbs. They wanted me to take a walk out in the hall, regardless of how much pain I was in. Whenever I stopped to take a breath, one of them would try to push me in order to keep moving. After the third push, I turned around and pushed him back. He got up off the floor yelling, "Mr. King I was only trying to help you!" He was actually making me lose my balance.

I shared a room with a ninety-year old man who seemed to be at peace. During four of the six days of my hospital stay, he just lay there and either stared at me while I cried or watched television. The nurses and doctors often complained because he refused to eat the hospital food. "It just don't taste right!" he yelled. I could tell that he ate whatever he wanted, and no one ever disputed with him about it.

"Can you please eat something sir?" they begged.

He'd sample some of the food then blurt out, "Aach... tastes like shit!" I laughed so hard I lost my breath.

The day before he was released, a doctor asked him about his eating habits. "Oh, I eats!" he declared and gave a rundown of what he ate on a daily basis. "In da mornin I eats two eggs wit bacon, grits an' two pieces of toast...

an' I use butta... none o'dat margareene... BUTTA!" The doctor stared in awe as he continued. "Fo lunch, I eats a balony sammich or two wit some orange pop. Fo dinna, I eats fried chicken or pork chops or steak... whateva meat I want... wit corn, mash potatas, beans, greens... like I said, I eats!"

The doctor told him how all that food was hurting him and suggested a meal plan for him to follow. Before the doctor could continue the old man barked, "Dammit I ain't got time fo aw dat! Imma eat wut I like, when I like!"

"But sir," the doctor pleaded.

"But nuttin!!! I'm too old to be changin' shit! Don't worry 'bout me, save dat boy's life!!!" the old man yelled.

The doctor shook his head as he walked out the room. The old man glared at me for a second, then turned his head to look at the television. I stared at him for a minute, then dozed off.

He didn't talk to me until the day he was released. As he got dressed he paused, glanced at me and said, "Son aw dat cryin' ain't worth shit if you ain't doin nuttin' bout it!" He shook his head and huffed, "Boy ya young... you ain't begun to live. I'm ninety... I dun been 'round da world, dun fought wars, had nice cars, ya name it... I DID IT!" I stared at him as he put his shoes on, amazed that he didn't need any help with anything.

He continued to ramble until his ride came. In the midst of my sleep apnea sessions, I tried to take in everything he said. I could've sworn he said that this hospital stay was his first one in fifty years.

"Dey tryna make me take aw dis medicine... I ain't takin' shit!!!" he barked as he walked to the door.

Before he left he said, "Son lose sum o dat weight, find you a nice gurl and make a few babies. You got cha whole life head o ya... don't let nuttin' hold ya back! Take care son." He smiled at me and nodded his head as he walked out the door. I smiled back, realizing it was the first time I'd smiled in weeks.

After the old man left, I just lay there and thought about what he said and what to do with my life if God gave me the chance to live. I tried not to cry, but I couldn't fight it. I felt so weak. I thought about my niece Makenna, who was barely four months old, thinking I would never get the chance to watch her grow up. I cried even harder because I would never get the chance at being a father.

By the middle of the week, a doctor came in the room and told me about gastric bypass surgery that would help me lose weight. "Mr. King, you qualify for this operation. We can have you ready and sent to St. Vincent by tomorrow" he said. While he continued to talk, I cut him off saying that I had to think about this. I'd never had surgery before, or at least as far as I could remember, and I'd heard so many stories of people dying under the knife. He gave me a card and told me to give him a call when I was ready. I decided that it wasn't for me, then balled the card up and threw it towards the garbage can.

KONKERER

The next day, which was a Thursday, a nurse came in and told me they were releasing me. "Sir, there's nothing we can do for you, so we're sending you home. If we find out what's wrong with you, we'll call you." I honestly didn't care if they called me or not, as long as I got the hell out of there. While I was getting dressed, I noticed my clothes had gotten a little tighter. I didn't care, I was ready to go. I called my mother and asked her to pick me up.

On the way home, my mom felt something was wrong because I looked larger than I did going into the hospital. The whole ride home and in the house, my mother just shook her head. I think the medicine also made me paranoid because I thought she couldn't stand to look at me anymore. The next morning, the doctor called and told me that I was diagnosed with congestive heart failure, COPD and bronchitis. He prescribed a steroid pill and breathing mist for bronchitis, an iron pill, Lasix for swelling and some kind of heart medicine.

That weekend seemed to be full of trial, error and embarrassment. I couldn't move around much; it took five to ten minutes to walk from the bedroom to the bathroom. I knew I needed help, but I was being stubborn. I did a lot of crying because I couldn't understand how I could go from running, to barely being able to walk, within weeks.

My aunt Julie (who was fighting breast cancer at that time), walked into the room. She looked at me for a brief moment then ran out saying, "Ooh Bobby, I'm not used to you just laying there looking all weak like that! You're not weak! That's not you! Where's the Bobby I'm used to?!"

All I could do was lay there and cry. She wasn't letting the cancer get the best of her, and she wanted me to be the same way. I admired her strength. My feelings of embarrassment didn't set in until Monday, when I needed Stef to help me wash up.

As he washed me down, he kept trying to convince me to go back to the hospital. I just ignored him. He would often blurt out, "Oh my God!" He couldn't believe how swollen I was. When I say that everything was swollen, I mean everything! My crotch had gotten so swollen that it caused my feet to be three to four feet apart while standing. He screamed, "Oh my God! Bob, you gotta go back to the hospital! Please, do it for me?!" I just looked at him. He didn't have to wash me down, but that's what brothers do. I will always love and admire him for that.

The next day, a nurse came by to visit and see how I was doing. She was the only nurse that seemed to actually care about me. She even told me that she had a very large son. After asking me several questions about my health, she suggested that I go back to the hospital. I simply told her "NO!" All I could think about was how nasty those nurses were to me.

She kneeled down, squeezed my ankles and said, "You see that indentation in your legs? That's Type II Edema. Your body is filled with fluid."

"Okay... and?" I thought.

She put her hand on her hips and shouted out, "Robert, don't you want to live?"

"Uh... yeah" I replied sarcastically.

She squeezed my ankles again and said, "At this stage, I'll give you two weeks."

I told her "I don't need two weeks... I'm not going back to the hospital." Yes, I was being stubborn.

She glared at me and said, "I'm not talking about that, I'm talking about you not living."

I sighed deeply and said, "Alright, I'll go back!" She stepped out the room to talk to my mother and call the hospital. She promised she would make sure that I would get treated better. She kept her promise.

This time, the fire department came instead of the paramedics. Even though they made me walk from the back bedroom to the front door and down the stairs, they let me take several rest breaks. All in all, they made me feel a lot better than before. This time, it was during the day and it seemed like all my neighbors were outside. Out of embarrassment, I kept my eyes shut.

On my way to the hospital, I started to feel a sense of security. This time, my mom stayed with me in the ER to make sure I was being well taken care of. She left later that night when she knew I was okay. Throughout the first night, I just lay there thinking. For the first time, I was actually able to pray and ask the Lord for guidance. From there, I put it all in His hands.

The next morning, three nurses came in to bathe and weigh me. The weigh-in showed that I had gained almost 50 lbs. of fluid. The first doctor's wrong diagnosis and prescriptions had made my condition worse. After several tests, my new doctor prescribed the proper medicine and I started to lose weight in fluid. Not only was I immediately starting to feel better, I also could breathe easier.

Later that day, my mother came back to the hospital. She brought me a CD player and a day-to-day bible. Each morning, I would read the daily scriptures and take a walk down the hall and back to my room. One of the nurses gave me some paper and a pen so I could draw and write. Each day seemed to get better and my health was improving. The only issues I had were finding out that there was a possibility that I was unable to have children, and getting a bed sore on my lower back.

After staying in the hospital for about three weeks, I was sent to a rehabilitation center in Andover, Ohio right after my release. Even though the center helped me get back on my feet and regain my strength, I left after three weeks. My brother Stef felt I should've stayed there longer, but I felt it had served its purpose. Believe me, I am forever grateful to that center, but some of the things that went on there just did not sit right with me.

KONKERER

There were a lot of morbidly obese people that seemed to be just living there and not taking advantage of what the center had to offer. They either refused to go to their physical therapy sessions, chain smoked, or wouldn't follow the center's diet plans... some did all of the above. It amazed me to see some of them ordering food from various restaurants and none of the center's staff would do anything about it. I just shook my head and moved forward with the program.

During my stay at the center, my father called me to see how I was doing. It was the first time we had talked in months. He was upset to find out that I had been in the hospital for weeks and didn't give him a call. I wasn't going to call him either. I was mad at him for a lot of reasons. YES, I am stubborn, and I got it from HIM.

CHAPTER 12
Building a Blessing

When I got home from the rehabilitation center, I wasted no time trying to get back into college. I received a letter in the mail stating that I was placed on academic suspension for dropping out. I immediately appealed, showing proof that my reasons for dropping out were legitimate. After further investigation, the suspension was lifted, allowing me to return to school in the fall. During my hiatus from school, I spent a lot of time over my father's house. We would just sit around drinking coffee and having endless conversations. We didn't always see things eye-to-eye, but we enjoyed each other's company.

For a brief moment, our conversations became a little emotional. We talked about how our relationship was in the past, which allowed me to tell him how cruel he was. It was the first time I was able to tell him how I really felt without him going off. I remember how he just sat there with this look of confusion on his face. "Was I really that bad?" he asked. I nodded yes.

After a moment of silence, he looked at me and said, "Bobby I love ya... I raised you the best way I could." Oddly enough, I believed him.

My mom often told me how his mother raised him... beat the hell out of him then asked questions later. He went through the same mental abuse. He rarely saw his father and longed for that "father and son" relationship. You would think that he would've made an attempt to do the opposite when raising us. My mother often reminded me that we had to break those chains... the sins of generations past. Before I could even do that, I had to learn how to forgive, which was a grueling process, especially when the enemy was constantly lurking around and spewing his venom on my progression.

On January 11, 2002, my aunt Julie died due to complications resulting from the cancer. The day after she died, I sat on the floor listening to music while writing a poem in her honor. One of the songs I was listening to made me so emotional that I burst into tears. "They keep leaving me!" I cried out. My brother Stef ran in and hugged me. He didn't know what I was talking about. You see, in the span of eleven years I'd lost my grandfather, my grandmother and my aunt, and at that very moment it hit me. They were my biggest fans and they saw things in me that I couldn't see. Before my aunt Julie died, she made me promise to lose weight, live healthy and share my talents. I believe she's proud of me.

While in college, I had the honor of volunteering as a mentor at Mayfair Elementary. Twice a week I would go to a classroom of boys, help them with their school work and conduct random conversations. I found it odd that they had more respect for me than their teacher. It's amazing that I see a few of those boys every now and then. They're grown and in college. Makes me feel like a proud father.

One day while sitting in the bar, a man walked up to me and said, "Yo, can I talk to you for a minute?" I looked up at him and said, "Wassup?"

He said, "Man I got some gear your size... slick shit! I'm talkin' dress suits, dress shirts, jeans, polo shirts, joggin' suits... like I said... slick shit. I'll give you a good price and you can have it all." I told him I'd think about it. In E.C., niggas have motives... I'm just saying. He introduced himself as Nick, gave me his pager number and said, "Yo, hit me up!" While I was looking at his number I thought to myself, "It is 2002, who the hell has a pager?"

A few days later he came back to the bar, walked up to me and said, "Yo, I'm serious about that gear!"

I looked up at him and said, "Dude, what's up with you? You seem suspect!"

For a brief moment he stared at me with a look of confusion and then said, "Yo, I'm serious. Look, I've been blessed. I had the gastric bypass operation six months ago. I was your size. Since I'm losing all this weight, I don't need the clothes anymore." I told him that I was considering that operation. He stood up and said, "Do it! It's a blessing... a new lease on life." As he walked away he said, "Hit me up!"

The gastric bypass operation is a procedure that minimizes the size of your stomach so you eat less; thus, allowing you to lose weight. I used to think that having that process done meant that you were too lazy to do it on your own. In order to even be qualified for it, you had to be 100 lbs. overweight. Can you believe there are people trying to gain that extra twenty or 30 lbs. just to get it? Sickening.

A week later Nick came into the bar, looked at me and said, "Yo, I haven't heard from you!" I told him that I was going to call and that I'd had a busy week. He sat down and said, "Yo I'll tell you what, you can have the gear... you don't have to pay me nothing. Like I said, I've been blessed and I'm passing the blessing off to you my brother."

I looked at him and said, "Thanks, man!" He gave me the name of his doctor and told me to call him.

KONKERER

As he walked away, he turned around and said, "Yo get that operation then pass the blessing on to someone else. Call me tomorrow, I'm serious! Call me tomorrow and come and get this slick shit bruh!"

I replied, "Okay, okay!"

The next day I paged him three times and he didn't call back. I paged him every day for about a week... still, no call. It seemed like he had fallen off the face of the earth. On Sunday, I got a call from a woman asking if someone had paged her. I told her that I was paging Nick and apologized. "I'm his wife" she replied. I asked if I could speak to him and she told me that he had just died.

"What?! How?!" I asked.

She explained that someone broke into their house and shot him. "Damn, I'm so sorry. Is it okay if I come to the funeral?" I asked.

She paused for a minute then started yelling, "I don't know you! You could be the one who shot my husband! You might be trying to come back to find what you're looking for!"

I snapped back, "Whoa, whoa, ma'am! I'm just a guy he befriended a few weeks ago. He told me that he was blessed with the weight loss operation months ago, and he wanted to pass the blessing by giving me the clothes he couldn't fit anymore."

After a brief pause she mumbled, "Sounds like my Nick... always tryin' to help someone." I told her that he was a cool guy. She replied, "Yes, he really was young man... bye!"

A few months after Nick died, I started to take the operation into consideration. I called the hospital where Nick said his doctor worked at but was redirected to another doctor that specialized in the procedure. This doctor seemed to be on point and willing to help me. He sent me to physical and mental evaluations along with several support sessions. He later came to the conclusion that I was too large for his equipment, and I needed to lose 160 lbs. to meet their weight limit.

I got furious. There was no way that I would be able to lose all that weight. I asked him why he sent me to all those sessions and evaluations if he knew that I was over the weight limit. "It's a part of the procedure" he answered.

"Thanks for nothing!" I growled.

When I mentioned the doctor Nick referred me to, he chuckled and said, "Oh yeah he'll do it, but I wouldn't recommend him." I just got up and walked out of the office.

Before I decided to call Nick's doctor, I researched and contacted several other medical centers that specialized in the surgery. Each one of them gave me the same run around. Nick's doctor was my last resort. I called the doctor and set an appointment for December 11, 2002.

KONKERER

The day before the appointment, I had an uneasy feeling. I prayed that this wouldn't be a waste of my time. I also thought about how the other doctor chuckled. My mind started racing because I didn't know what to expect.

When I walked into the doctor's office, he greeted me with a firm handshake and said, "Welcome Mr. King." After we sat down, I told him that Nick referred me to him. He nodded his head then sighed, "It was very sad to hear about his death." I told him how Nick professed that this procedure was a blessing and it would be for me also. He nodded again, then asked me what I was expecting from this operation. I told him that I was doing this for my health. He smiled and said, "Indeed."

As he looked over my files, he noticed that I had been rejected by one of his colleagues, then asked how I felt about it. I told him that it seemed like they were giving me the run around.

"Well, all of the evaluations and support sessions were a part of the procedure. You won't have to worry about dealing with that part again" he said.

I asked him if I would be the largest person he's performed the procedure on. He answered, "Oh no, the largest person I've operated on was 1,100 lbs." "Geesh!" I yelped. "I see why your colleagues chuckled when I mentioned your name, you don't have a weight limit" I said.

"Well Mr. King, my colleagues believe my style is a little unorthodox. They set limits for themselves where I have none" he replied. After leaving the doctor's office, I felt at ease.

On February 23, 2003, the doctor called and told me that the operation date was on April 26th. I was so happy. The only problem with the date was that I couldn't participate in my cousin's wedding and my graduation was a month later on May 31st. It didn't matter though, I had a mission.

The morning of the operation, I was starving because I couldn't eat anything the day before. My mother and cousin Lisa stayed with me for support. We all talked and joked around as the nurses prepared me for the surgery. The next thing I knew, I was in "la la" land.

When I woke up, I could hardly breathe because there were tubes lodged in my throat and nose. I remember the nurses yelling, "Calm down Mr. King... breathe slowly!"

I was later taken to the recovery room and was accompanied by my mother, Lisa and a few nurses. I was heavily drugged and couldn't feel a thing. My throat was really dry, so the nurse would have me suck on a bubble gum flavored sponge. I started acting silly by constantly telling the nurse to "wet my whistle." I was in good spirits.

The first two nights I was heavily drugged, and I couldn't stay awake while my family visited. I can remember opening my eyes a few times and noticing that my father and brother Stef were there. Several times during my stay at the hospital, I got up to walk around. By Thursday, I was discharged. An hour after I got home, two physical therapists came over and made me take a walk up and down my street.

During my healing period, I caught an infection which is common with very large wounds. That was a crazy experience. I remember noticing a bubble protruding from my scar. When the nurse came over for his weekly visit, he took a swab and poked it several times. Soon after, it erupted with a greenish- yellow fluid that smelled terrible. "What the hell is that?" I yelled.

"Well Mr. King, you've caught an infection... nothing serious" he replied. He taught me how to take care of my wound while he wasn't around. He also advised me to buy some Maxi Pads to absorb the infected fluid... um...err... yeah... so... anyway... they worked very well.

I'd like to thank you Dr. Udekwu, for helping me out when other surgeons turned me down. Thank you Nick for passing the blessing... rest in peace my friend. From the gastric bypass surgery I've lost a little over 300 lbs. I've gained some of it back though... um... err... long story.

CHAPTER 13
Poetic Newness

    Several months after my aunt Julie passed, my life started to take a turn for the better. My health was improving, and I was two semesters away from achieving my Bachelor's in Business Management. Even though I was still going to the bar and hanging around the same circle of people, I was looking for something different to do with my life. My cousin Gwen mentioned an open mic poetry thing happening every Sunday at a coffee shop in Warrensville. I decided to go check it out a few weeks later.

I remember my first visit like it was yesterday. As soon as I walked in, I was engulfed by the aroma of incense and coffee. There was another doorway full of hanging beads like from the '70s. As I made my way through, I expected the atmosphere to be full of nappy dreads, finger snaps and the sounds of bongo drums being played. But to my surprise, I saw something completely different.

I noticed that I was one of the first customers there, so I sat in the back on one of the oversized bamboo chairs. A few minutes later, the owner of the coffee shop walked in, staring at me and taking several glances at the chair. "Damn, he acts like he's never seen a fat dude before!" I thought. He eased his way a little closer to me saying, "Be careful man. Those chairs aren't that strong." I just stared at him. While waiting for the festivities to begin, I noticed that the D.J. (Q-Nice) had a slight resemblance to Stokely from Mint Condition. Maybe it was because of his thin goatee and braids. The melody from "You Send Me Swingin" kept playing in my head.

Another dude (Jabaazz Snipes) walked up to me and said, "Hey, I remember you! You went to Warrensville. You used to draw graffiti on the bathroom walls!" I just laughed. As more people filled the room, Q-Nice and Jabaazz started hosting. They announced that they were co-founders of the group Chief Rocka Entertainment, then introduced several other members... Echo, Mad Poet, L.S. Royal and Sanches. They even had a first lady, Ebony Faith, who lived in California. I would often see her dancing on Soul Train.

As the night went on, Q and Jabaazz kept the audience entertained. As they introduced a new poet to the stage, I started to like poetry more and more. Everyone had their own style. Nothing like what I was used to, you know... different from Maya Angelou, Langston Hughes or even Robert Frost. By the end of the night, I was sold.

I went to the venue as often as I could, but I never had the urge to get on stage and share a poem. In April of 2003, I stopped going due to my gastric bypass operation. During the eight plus weeks I spent healing, I was sitting around writing and drawing. I was missing poetry and couldn't wait until I was able to go back. By the time I started again, there were two new additions to the group, Tom Noy and One Truth... 'The Twin Towers.'

As time passed, I got to know the members of C.R.E. and a host of other poets. I realized that One Truth, L.S., Mad Poet and I shared similar backgrounds... we're all from the hood... nuff said. I would often get bugged about getting on the mic. I noticed at the end of each show Q would say, "A poet is not only the one who stands to speak, but also the one who stands to listen." I started telling them, "I stand to listen!" I later wrote a poem using the same title.

I graduated from Myers University with a Bachelor of Science degree in Business Administration on May 31, 2003. I had finally reached a personal goal. The smile on my mother's face was priceless, because I felt like I'd let her down for getting kicked out of college as a kid. I was also glad that my father was able to attend my graduation.

I was the first on my mother's side of the family to achieve a Bachelor's degree. It inspired some of my family members to pursue their academic goals.

I brought in the 2004 New Year by attending Notre Dame College in pursuit of my teacher's license. I fulfilled the coursework and my student teaching at Cleveland Central Catholic and Jane Addams, but due to some personal and financial aid issues, I couldn't finish. I didn't fret; Lord willing, I'll get to handle that in the near future.

I also got a job working for a group home for at-risk boys from ages ten to seventeen; many of whom had been molested, and subsequently ended up being molesters. It was important they realized there was a MAN that truly cared for them, and I encouraged them that they could be anything they wanted to be. What I didn't like about the group home was that the staff constantly reminded them that they were sexual offenders. I believed that wouldn't motivate them to do better. With the other staff members working against me, I decided to leave after four months.

On February 22, 2004 (my aunt Julie's birthday), I decided to take that leap and read a poem. I hesitated for a while before I signed the list. I was trying to think of a stage name... I had nothing. By the time I got to the table to sign the list, I wrote the first thing that came to my mind... 'Frost'... a graffiti alias I'd used in high school.

I was so nervous. I started debating if I should go on and read or take my name off the list. L.S. was hosting that night. When he called my name, I waited a few seconds before I got up. "I guess Frost isn't here" he said. I finally got up and made my way to the stage. He noticed that it was my first time, so he had everyone stand up. By the time I got to the stage, my left leg wouldn't stop shaking. I wondered if the audience noticed. I announced that it was my aunt's birthday, and to pay homage to her I wanted to read the poem I wrote for her funeral. After that day, I started reading more. I even started singing and sharing my artwork.

At the end of 2004, Q asked me if I would be interested in being a part of C.R.E.'s street team; I accepted. The street team consisted of C.O., Songchild, Zion Venia, Suspicious and me. We went anywhere and everywhere, distributing flyers and promoting The Vibe Session and Lyrical Rhythms. It was cool to be a part of something different from the norm. By 2006, I took on more responsibilities for the company which included promoting, event planning, designing flyers and security, as well as being a performance poet. For a moment, I couldn't go anywhere without hearing, "Hey Frost!" or "Hey, aren't you Q-Nice's bodyguard?" Very funny.

Being on the scene sparked some new opportunities for me. While accompanying Q at an event he was hosting, I was offered a job for a company that provided security and bodyguard services. My detail included bouncing at a few clubs, when needed, and accompanying local and national celebrities throughout the day before their performance. After two years my boss got arrested for money laundering, so I started my own security business and worked at several clubs around Cleveland.

Another blessing for me was my graphics business that just fell into my lap. I first named my company Frostbyte Grafix, then decided to change it to Syre Grafix in honor of my father after he passed. I was already designing for C.R.E. and people liked my work. I started designing and printing flyers, business cards and logos. In a year, I found myself working until 3 a.m. in the morning. I wasn't trying to compete with the likes of Hot Cards or Jak Prints; I was just happy making a living doing something I loved. After a few years, I got burned out from printing and just focused on the designing.

My graphics company is now serving clients in California, Washington DC, Maryland, New York, New Jersey and North Carolina. I was blessed with the honor of designing for the Individual World Poetry Slam, local performing artists, the Cleveland Free Clinic, Tri-C, Greater Is He Publishing, and a host of large and small businesses. My father saw my work and said, "Bobby, you need to forget about teaching and focus on starting a graphics business!"

I laughed and told him, "Man, you are so late!" He looked at me and smiled. I knew he was proud of me. He didn't have to say a word.

Thanks to C.R.E., I've had the pleasure of performing on various stages throughout the country, and once performed in Toronto. I guess that makes me an International Poet. I've traveled to different cities to support the Cleveland Slam Team. I've met and befriended many artists throughout the country.

I've also become a mentor and motivational speaker, spending endless hours mentoring teens and young adults who have been affected by child abuse, rape, drugs and alcohol, etc. I help them realize that no matter what they've been through, their broken pasts don't have to dictate their futures. I'm also teaching them how to forgive. My grandmother would be so proud of me.

While Chief Rocka Entertainment grew as a business, I decided to pursue an MBA in Business Administration at the University of Phoenix. I also tried to utilize what I learned to help C.R.E flourish. There were so many things working against me during that period, but I kept the faith and worked hard. I graduated in 2009 with a GPA of 3.4. My goal is to become a college professor.

CONCLUSION

By 2009, my father and I had the relationship I'd always longed for. We would drink coffee and talk for hours. His house was always open to me no matter how late it was. He yelled at me for pulling into his driveway to get some rest after a late night of doing security. If he didn't hear from me, he'd call just to say, "Hey Bobby, where you been? Why don't you come over and have a cup of coffee!" I'd be there in no time. The one thing I had longed to hear from him finally gave me a sense of pride... he told me he was proud of me.

When I gave him a copy of my first book *Frostbytten*, he smiled and said, "My boy is an author!" I told him that I was working on this book and he gave me his blessing. He told me that he hopes it gets to help others.

In one of our last conversations he said, "Bobby, ever since you was four years old you always had a better idea. That's what makes you unique." He wanted me to buy a foreclosed house on his street. I imagined him coming over, riding in his scooter just to supervise while I made repairs to it.

On October 12, 2009, my father passed away due to heart complications. I was so upset with myself because I had an opportunity to see him the day before while leaving a dear friend's baby shower in Twinsburg. I was getting prepared to see him when I received the call from my sister. I got mad at him for leaving me. I wasn't ready for him to go. Eight years of a renewed relationship was not enough, but it outweighed the many years of pain, anger and hate.

I will miss him dearly and will forever cherish everything I've learned from him. My friend, Brandy Rankins, blessed me with a chance to feature on her track entitled "Memories I Hold Close." (http://www.reverbnation.com/brandywine01/songs). I even had a chance to re-enact a telephone conversation on the track. I pray that I continue to make him and my mother proud of me in the years to come, because everything I am comes from the Lord, and them.

This is my story... my testimony. The Lord carried me through all my storms and fought all my battles. He showed me that there's nothing to fear. During my time of weakness, he reformed me and made me stronger mentally and spiritually. All bitterness erased. I can stand in front of the world proud to be a Man of God... a Man of Destiny. I'm more than a Konkerer.

A MESSAGE TO THE READER:

First off, I'd like to thank you for purchasing my book. I pray that you aren't offended by the foul language. By no means was this book made to bash my father or anyone else. I wrote this book to show you that I'm a product of God's work. Even when I was in my lowly stages and gave up on myself, He would bring angels into my life to encourage me to hold on to my faith and move forward. While writing this book, I realized that even though I was having problems with my father, there were many other men that took me under their wing and encouraged me. I am forever grateful to God for bringing them into my life.

There's no reason to complain about all the closed doors and failed opportunities, because He's opened new ones and is continually blessing me with opportunities I never thought were possible. While finishing this book, I didn't realize all the accomplishments I've made or the lives I've touched. It was all Him.

This is my testimony. I'm happy and I love myself. I may not be as physically strong as I was back then, but I'm strong mentally and spiritually. I realized that I had to learn to forgive myself as well as forgive those who've hurt me. I'm continually forgiving... because of my size, people can be so cruel. My mission is not to get angry every time someone crosses me, but to continue loving and letting my light shine.

I may not mentor young adults, visit schools or conduct motivational speaking events as much as I used to, but I continue to encourage others as much as possible through my work, my blog site (www.frostbyte76.blogspot.com) or other forms of social media.

I am a blessed man... a Konkerer, if you will... and so are you.

When you're done reading this book, please share it with your family and friends, especially those that are dealing with certain issues.

Thank you very much, and God bless.

Live, Love & Forgive

Robb 'FrostByte' King

ABOUT THE AUTHOR

Robb FrostByte King is a Poet / Author / Teacher / Artist / Singer / Security Guard, etc. A "Jack-of-All-Trades" by nature.

He's a lover of art and music. His poetry is eclectic. His goal is to make you laugh while giving you something to think about.

He's a former member of Chief Rocka Entertainment. His mission as a member of C.R.E. was to be more than just a performance poet. He has worked hard to be a driving force in Cleveland through networking, and supporting other venues and events.

He believes in keeping the arts alive in Cleveland, and wants everyone to keep supporting. His first chapbook "*FrostBytten*" is full of poems, haikus, short stories, and art that has gotten rave reviews by his peers and others in the entertainment industry. Currently, you may catch him at an open mic venue near you, either singing or reciting poetry.

Robb is a freelance Graphic Designer for his own company, Syre Grafix, and has an MBA in Business Administration. His goal is to become a College Professor.

www.ingramcontent.com/pod-product-compliance
Lightning Source LLC
Chambersburg PA
CBHW071142090426
42736CB00012B/2199